The life and times of post-modernity

'Postmodernity' is often claimed as the great transformation in society and culture. But is it? In this book Keith Tester casts a cautious eye on such grandiose claims. Tester draws on a series of themes and stories from European sociology and literature to show that many of the great statements from 'postmodernity' are misplaced. 'Postmodernity' is not the harbinger or expression of a new world. It is a reflection of the unresolved paradoxes and possibilities of modernity; 'postmodernity' is wholly parasitic. The author establishes a clearly expressed and stimulating model of modernity to demonstrate the stakes and consequences of 'postmodernity'. This book uses a wealth of sources which are usually denigrated or ignored in the debates on 'postmodernity'. As such it sheds new light on old claims. But it never fails to acknowledge the profound insights of sociologists and other authors. *The Life and Times of Post-Modernity* is a continuation of the themes which Tester raised in his earlier books with Routledge, *The Two Sovereigns* and *Civil Society*.

Keith Tester lectures in Sociology and Cultural Studies at the University of Portsmouth.

The life and times of post-modernity

Keith Tester

London and New York

First published 1993
by Routledge
11 New Fetter Lane, London EC4P 4EE

Simultaneously published in the USA and Canada
by Routledge
29 West 35th Street, New York, NY 10001

© 1993   Keith Tester

Typeset in Times by
NWL Editorial Services, Langport, Somerset

Printed and bound in Great Britain by
T.J. Press (Padstow) Ltd, Padstow, Cornwall

British Library Cataloguing in Publication Data
A catalogue record for this book is available from the British
Library

Library of Congress Cataloging in Publication Data
A catalog record for this book is available from the Library of
Congress

ISBN 0–415–07545–9   0–415–09832–7 (pbk)

Contents

Introduction

'A fine setting for a fit of despair,' it occurred to him, 'if I were only standing here by accident instead of design'.

Franz Kafka

The real dwelling plight lies in this, that mortals ever search anew for the essence of dwelling, that they *must ever learn to dwell*.

Martin Heidegger

... to be absolutely modern means to be the ally of one's grave diggers.

Milan Kundera

In two of my earlier books, *The Two Sovereigns* and *Civil Society*, I tried to come to terms with some of the hopes and disasters of European modernity. In particular, I tried to provide some thoughts on why the enterprises of modernity always seemed to burst into flames, or just dissipate into irrelevance, at more or less precisely the moment when their realization seemed to have become a distinct possibility.

It was implicit to the assumptions of those essays that to be writing about modernity as an item of interest rather than as a universally lived, experienced and inhabited condition, meant that I was not self-evidently and easily within the boundaries of the modern. I was, so to speak, without its bounds. But to some extent, I must have been within the boundaries of something to be able to know that I was outside the boundaries of something else. As such, it might be said that this book is concerned with the conditions which constitute the ground from which it is possible to see modernity.

In this book, I have tried to provide a clearer picture of my interpretation of the condition from which I was perceiving modernity. With this book, I have tried to go a little way towards upholding the maxim of Alvin Gouldner and put the cameraman back into the picture. It is up to you to decide whether the picture is clear and interesting or so out of focus as to be incoherent.

Consequently, this book is concerned with some of the hermeneutic stakes and conditions of possibility of the debates on modernity and, for that matter, post-modernity itself. However, I hope that this book is of more than autobiographical importance (I hope it is about more than one lone cameraman). After all, I am a sociologist and I struggle to practise something called sociology. And as a good sociologist, I assume that I inhabit along with numerous others a specific kind of social and cultural milieu. I am not an isolated, Robinson Crusoe type of figure who stands apart from the world. To understand you and I is, in the first instance, to understand the relationships which together make us what we are. Consequently, this book is about social and cultural worlds. It is not at all about entirely personal events.

In these ways then, *The Life and Times of Post-modernity* represents an attempt to think beyond the terrain which was mapped in *The Two Sovereigns* and *Civil Society*. Part of that 'thinking beyond' has meant that I am now much less enthusiastic about the possibilities and implications of post-modernity than I was in the earlier books (and even then, my enthusiasm was always tempered by a niggling doubt about some of the great claims which had been made for post-modernity).

However, *The Life and Times of Post-modernity* does have some things in common with the other two books. Not least, like the other efforts *The Life and Times of Post-modernity* is explicitly an essay in interpretation. In many ways, it is a speculation. Once again, this book does not pretend to give the right answers, and neither does it pretend to contain the keys to the ultimate truth. I would not even pretend that it necessarily asks all the most pertinent questions, although I hope that it raises interesting and useful problems. The book is simply an essay which attempts to work out why the kinds of people who write and read about post-modernity (people like you and I) seem to see the world in some ways as opposed to others.

I know that these largely hermeneutic interests might well leave my work (if that phrase is not too pompous) open to a number of criticisms. In many ways, that is something to be accepted if not actively encouraged; after all, the kind of sociology I am engaged in is about proposing alternative ways of seeing without offering a best or only alternative. However, it seems to me to be worth spending a little time considering the potential criticism that this book, just like *The Two Sovereigns* and *Civil Society*, represents a writing of the world which pays little or no attention to what happens in 'real life'. It could be said that I have a tendency to reduce the world to the status of a writing and a reading, when I should be more concerned with the reflection on practices in and of the world (that is, I reduce everything to ideas rather than to material actions and circumstances).

I suppose this criticism is to some degree encouraged by my tendency to seemingly eschew the orthodox stage props of sociological justification and instead, to engage in a dialogue with authors. I talk about other books so frequently, and tend to draw my 'evidence' from them for two reasons. Firstly, novels are so much more interesting and profound than most pieces of sociology. They are definitely much better written. This is a largely aesthetic justification. Secondly, there is a moral reason which has been stressed by Richard Rorty. Rorty says that 'the novel, the movie, and the TV program have, gradually but steadily, replaced the sermon and the treatise as the principal vehicles of moral change and progress' (Rorty 1989: xvi). According to Rorty then, moral progress and the signposts to the 'Ways Forward' are not to be found in the products of academia (therefore they are not to be found in this book). Instead, they are to be found in other kinds of cultural production. Unfortunately, I know little of the cinema and good television and so I can only refer to that world (literature) which is a little less mysterious to me. In other words, I am trying to work in the light of Richard Rorty's position although I do have doubts over the usefulness of notions like 'moral progress' (however liberally and decently the progress might be defined).

Basically, I am trying to unravel the meaning of the myths which support and constitute our societal and social reality. Mary Douglas has usefully defined myth as 'a contemplation of the unsatisfactory compromises which, after all, compose social life'. Douglas continues: 'In the devious statements of the myth, people can recognize indirectly what it would be difficult to admit openly and yet what is patently clear to all and sundry, that the ideal is not attainable' (Douglas 1975: 156). A myth is a story which mediates and comes to terms with the conflicts and difficulties of societal and social existence. Myth contemplates the difficulties of our lives and either reconciles them in some way or pushes them outside of the milieu of the things which need to be said. Moreover, myth can provide explanations of why the ideals which we so often uphold with such great faith, commitment and enthusiasm are never attained; myth helps us come to terms with our seemingly endless failures.

In my last couple of books I have been trying to show how modernity was interpreted through a series of myths (myths called 'Society' or 'Communism' or 'Freedom' or whatever; myths which were often justified through the proclaimed scientificity of 'Classical Sociology' and 'Social Science') which could, and to some considerable extent actually did, make sense. Instead of accepting those myths at face value I have struggled to interpret their stakes, implications, and their conditions of possibility. To concentrate on the writings of our world is actually to concentrate on the myths of our world; it is to explore the stories by which compromises are made, practical activities are justified and failures accepted. The concentration on the writings of the world (and indeed, the carrying out of a kind of sociology which is also in its own very modest way a writing), helps to develop an appreciation of what it actually means to exist and even fail in a social and a societal milieu. Such an emphasis can also help explain why the world is so commonly experienced and interpreted as a bounded place.

What all of this means is that this book is one which will hopefully be written by you in your reading of it. This text is one to be challenged; I hope it leads to you asking questions and providing answers for yourself. I also hope that the book goes a little way towards doing what all reflexive and interpretive sociology should do (but perhaps does not do often enough; this kind of sociology has had to live too often in the shadow of its siblings: legislative sociology and plain boring sociology). I hope that in a small way *The Life and Times of Post-modernity* will contribute to a multiplication of the meanings of the world so that we can make the world for ourselves without someone else telling us that they know what is really for the best. Those aims and hopes are very modest. If the post-modern intellectual should learn anything from modernity (and it is my fate to be a post-modern intellectual despite my reservations over what post-modernity might imply), it is the lesson of humility. More specifically, I would like to think that this book does not assist the belief that simply because something is incomprehensible to us it therefore does not have the right to exist.

This book is about living in a social and a cultural milieu, and the book itself is the product of social and cultural relationships. All my attempts to write something interesting have benefited enormously from the time and help unselfishly given by a small community of partners in my readings and writings. Consequently, and once again, I wish to express my continuing profound debts to Linda Rutherford and Zygmunt Bauman. Chris Rojek and Anne Gee continue to make sure that it is a pleasurable and fruitful experience to work for Routledge. They have all helped me in very different but equally important ways. But that does not mean that they would necessarily wish to be associated with a single word in this essay (I imagine that at least one of the people I have thanked would very strongly disagree with this book).

Chapter 1

Bounds

Georg Simmel once began a book with words which seem to be an entirely appropriate way of beginning this book as well. He wrote that: 'Man's position in the world is defined by the fact that in every dimension of his being and his behavior he stands at every moment between two boundaries' (Simmel 1971: 353). Georg Simmel continued to briefly outline what he meant when he spoke of these boundaries. Perhaps inevitably he saw the boundaries which define the position of the human in the world, the boundaries which give the human a place and a direction, in terms of a series of dichotomies; higher and lower, greater and lesser, better and worse (however, it must be admitted that Simmel seems a little vague as to the basis and the precise meaning of that human being and community). But without these polar opposites and without their ability to locate the human and to make sense of activities and institutions, the world would be more or less (another dichotomy) meaningless to us. After all, 'The boundary, above and below, is our means for finding direction in the infinite space of our worlds' (Simmel 1971: 353).

Without bounds, the human would be lacking in any ability to find direction in the world. Indeed, neither would the human be able to find a place in it. In other words, according to Simmel, boundaries are something like the precondition of purposeful activity and understanding. Without boundaries, the 'space of our worlds' would indeed be infinite. It would swamp us and stun us. As a corollary of that implication of boundlessness, without a definite place and a certain way of finding a direction, two of the most important possibilities which are fulfilled by boundaries, the world would be apprehended as absolutely immense. Consequently, the human would be defined as correspondingly small in relation to the infinite. The individual or for that matter the human species can only be big in the world if the limits of that world are placed firmly within fairly easy to understand conceptual and hermeneutic boundaries.

It seems to be the case that Simmel is hinting at a fundamentally aesthetic and a fundamentally Kantian view of things; without the boundaries which find place and locate the subjective agent of understanding, the human becomes small in relation to things. If you like, the human is a very small fish in a very big sea. Consequently, the things of the world are apprehended as sublime and, therefore, as possibly somewhat threatening. The boundaries not only find direction, as Simmel explicitly said, but they also lend security, hermeneutic certainty, and intelligibility. If you like, thanks to them the human is a potentially very big fish in a potentially very small sea. Boundaries make sure that the human does not have to confront the ambivalent sublimity of 'the infinite space of our worlds'.

Now it must be admitted that Georg Simmel is more than a little bit vague as to the status of these boundaries. He takes them as given and simply seeks to know of their implications. Certainly, Simmel explains that boundaries serve to make the world and the human and individual existence in the world intelligible. But he does not seem to explain where the boundaries come from. Simmel is unprepared to enter into the problem of whether boundaries are individual representations, societal constructions, representations of species-being, or indeed, whether they are to be understood as approximating with Ideas in Reason or a priori categories. Simmel does not spell out whether the boundaries are defining of the societal or whether the societal, on the contrary, is in one way or another defining of the boundaries. Instead, he simply takes boundaries and existence in the world as given and seeks to unravel the nature of the interplay between them.

Simmel makes the claim that the boundaries and the existent (what Simmel calls 'life') can only be understood through their coming together (in other words, and to use the terminology of a different tradition in sociological discourse, Simmel is perfectly sensibly refusing to fall into the trap of the debate between structure and agency). Simmel is in no doubt that without boundaries, life in the world (that is, existence) would be largely barren. It would definitely be largely incomprehensible. After all,

> participation in realities, tendencies, and ideas which involve a plus and a minus, a this side and a that side of our here and now . . . gives life two complementary, if often also contradictory, values: richness and determinacy.

> (Simmel 1971: 354)

Here, then, Simmel is saying that boundaries constitute so many attempts to *define* meanings, but the very existence and acceptance of the boundaries create firm ground (that is, given meanings), from which the social and societal can be *defining of itself*.

To be defined and to be self-defining are then two poles of the same continuum. Simmel writes that

> these continua, by which we are bounded and whose segments we ourselves bound, form a sort of coordinate system, through which, as it were, the locus of every part and content of our life may be identified.
>
> (Simmel 1971: 354)

Or, and to put the matter another way, without boundaries a book like this, which claims to offer interpretations of the social and the societal, actually could not say anything. But books like this, which are embedded in and which seek to move a little beyond, the boundaries of the existing sociological discourse, are indeed possible. That is to highlight not only a contradiction in the status of boundaries but, much more importantly, it is to hint at why social and cultural activity is taken by the participants to be constitutive of itself (culture understood as the product of previous culture). Basically, for Simmel it is important to realize that the existence of a boundary is, in principle, the actual precondition for a social or a cultural activity which might seek to go beyond the boundary.

As Georg Simmel said, 'the boundary is unconditional, in that its existence is constitutive of our given position in the world' (Simmel 1971: 354). But, and rather in contradiction to the unconditional, constitutive status of the boundary, it is also the case that 'no boundary is unconditional, since every one can on principle be altered, reached over, gotten around'. Bringing these two dimensions of the boundary together, the combination of the existence of the unconditional and yet the practice of the conditional, Simmel comes to the confident conclusion that 'this pair of statements appears as the explication of the inner unity of vital action' (Simmel 1971: 354). In other words, this is the philosopher's stone of social and cultural analysis.

So, according to Simmel, the boundaries which give direction to existence, and which locate that existence, are the precondition of their own transcendence. This is because, without boundaries, without direction and location, social and cultural activity would itself be a simply pointless thrashing about in the world. Without boundaries, social and cultural activity would have no form; it would be nothing more than amorphous content. As such, Simmel argues that the boundaries create forms, and the forms are the basis of meaning and interpretation. This point was made quite clearly by Simmel in his important essay on 'The Conflict in Modern Culture'. He suggests that the term culture refers to the process in which 'life produces certain forms in which it expresses and realizes itself; works of art, religions, sciences, technologies, laws, and innumerable others' (Simmel 1971: 375).

Culture can be said to imply all of those enterprises in which life might realize itself. But culture also implies the enterprises in which life is realized in bounded forms. Cultural products are themselves forms which make life intelligible: 'These forms encompass the flow of life and provide it with content and form, freedom and order' (Simmel 1971: 375). For example, thanks to the forms of modern art (say, cubism), we are now free to see the world in a different way. The continuity of that new way of seeing, of that new freedom (that is to say, its cultural longevity), is to some extent dependent on the extent to which the meanings and nature of cubism are established within boundaries (so that say, the cubist phase of Picasso can be identified readily and separated from his more conventionally figurative work). Freedom and order go together. Modern art established new forms which created new dimensions of life. But it could only do so if the forms of art took on a status independent of life (expressed in the principle of 'art for art's sake').

But whilst it is necessary to emphasize this dialectical relationship between culture as form and life as activity (life as the transcendence of boundaries), the implied permanence of the boundaries means that they stand apart from the activity which in principle constitutes them. Certainly, the boundaries create the space and the ground for social and cultural activity. But they can only perform those functions of the intimation of hermeneutic confidence if they are themselves to some extent taken for granted. The bounded forms are fixed; they establish the meaning of life. The boundaries make life meaningful. But, and this is a very important point, the very meaningfulness of life as something with a location and most significantly a direction (i.e. life as going somewhere other than here), implies the flow of life over permanent boundaries. That is, life is a process and a going beyond of the time and place fixed in forms. In relation to the hard and fast boundaries which make life intelligible, life is fluid.

The contradiction between fixation and fluidity is the essence of the conflict of modern culture which Simmel announced. Once again, Georg Simmel puts the matter very well:

These forms are frameworks for the creative life which, however, soon transcends them. The bounded forms acquire fixed identities, a logic and lawfulness of their own; this new rigidity inevitably places them at a distance from the spiritual dynamic which created them and which makes them independent.

(Simmel 1971: 375)

Form and life become distinct simply because life goes on whereas the forms established by the boundaries necessarily tend towards a degree of fixation. As such, the boundaries which make life intelligible are apprehended from the point of view of life as actually or potentially restraining. They are certainly understood as actually or potentially restrictive of freedom. As such, the boundaries are interpreted as manifesting tendencies towards reification.

An example of this dialectical conflict between life and form, between boundaries and transcendence, can be extracted from Georg Simmel's discussion of the boundaries of the form of time. Simmel makes the point that with the concept of time, life is divided into a series of bounded spheres called the past, the present and the future. Through time, life is given a direction; a before and an after, a greater and a lesser. Consequently, life is also harnessed to notions of history and process. Without the direction lent by the boundaries of time (yesterday, today, tomorrow), life would simply be a permanent and inescapable folding back of the same. Moreover, the bounded form of time operates in such a way that the label of reality can only be applied to those conditions and relationships which are of the present. But as Simmel explains, 'The present, in the strict logical sense of the term, does not encompass more than the absolute "unextendedness" of a moment. It is as little time as the point is space' (Simmel 1971: 359). In other words, the precise moment of the present is little more than a pin-prick in a far greater canvas. The present is always here and now (it is something like the sense which Eliot tried to grasp in his poem *Little Gidding*, when he reduced the world to the 'Now and in England'). But as soon as the present is conceived of as a moment in time, the situation changes rather a lot. Then, the present 'denotes merely the collision of past and future, which two alone make up time of any magnitude, that is real time. But since the one is no longer, and the other not yet, reality adheres to the present alone' (Simmel 1971: 359).

According to Georg Simmel then, time can be understood as a series of boundaries which can create the space for the identification and imposition of meaning in the world. Through the form of time, life is something which is intrinsically connected to process and to change. But, of course, whilst time makes sense of existence, that existence is not itself fully amenable to the rather mechanical rigidity of the boundaries. Once again, Simmel is trying to make the point that life actually transcends whatever boundaries might be applied to it. Whilst the form of time operates in such a way as to imply that reality is something only of the present and, therefore, itself somewhat outside of time (to some degree we are always 'Now and in England'), life means that reality is applied also to the past and to the future (by way of a simple example: today I know of the reality which is my yesterday).

In other words, there is a contradiction, a cultural conflict, between the formal status of reality as the fixed present, and the lived status of reality as inherently fluid. Simmel says of the fixed real: 'The subjectively *lived* life will not adjust to it. The latter feels itself, no matter whether logically justified or not, as something real in a temporal [i.e. fluid] dimension.' Simmel continues to provide an example of the conflict between the form and life. He says that everyday speech understands by the phrase 'the present', 'never the bare punctuality of its conceptual sense'. Rather everyday usage is 'always including a bit of the past and a somewhat smaller bit of the future' (Simmel 1971: 359).

Through the example of time then, it is possible for Georg Simmel to argue that life is transcendent in relation to the forms, the boundaries which make that life make sense. Indeed for Simmel, if life is not understood as transcendental, if it is not supposed that it overflows static boundary markers, culture would be experienced as an overwhelming oppression and life itself would be hardly worth living. The very fact that we can speak of boundaries as items of interest is taken by Simmel as a proof of the ability to go beyond boundaries, know them for what they are and thus make the world anew. But of course, the opportunities for global reconstruction are rather limited since, to know of the possibility of making the world for ourselves, we actually have to stand within bounds. 'Every limit is . . . transcended but of course only as a result of the fact that it is set, that is, that there exists something to transcend' (Simmel 1971: 358). The inside and the outside, the form and its transcendence cannot at all be separated. Rather, they only make sense if they are understood and analysed as the partners of a dialectic. As Simmel said, 'That we do not simply stand within these boundaries, but by virtue of our awareness of them have passed beyond them – this is the sole consideration which can save us from despair over them, our own limitations and finitude' (Simmel 1971: 358).

Here, when Simmel suggests that our ability to transcend the boundaries is more or less the only thing which saves us from a desolate despair over our imprisonment by them, there is more than a hint of panic.

After all, 'life can express itself and realize its freedom only through forms; yet forms must also necessarily suffocate life and obstruct freedom' (Simmel 1971: 391). Simmel knows the analytic and the intellectual case that life should be possessed of the ability to transcend the boundaries which give it direction and meaning (and which thereby seek to pin it down). But he is also aware of the actual case that the boundaries are increasingly apprehended as ossifications and reifications which are able to operate as extremely efficient prisons.

Whilst form and life should operate together in a dialectical conflict which nevertheless implies some creative synthesis, form and life in fact seem to move apart. The form defines life and as such, life is denied the ability to be defining of itself. Simmel knew that 'although these forms arise out of the life process, because of their unique constellation they do not share the restless rhythm of life, its ascent and descent, its constant renewal, its incessant divisions and reunifications' (Simmel 1971: 375). The boundaries are understood as increasingly tending to deny the legitimacy of the existence of that which is defined as incomprehensible, whereas life tends to involve the production of those incomprehensible things. Simmel's panic revolves around the possibility that eventually the inherent incomprehensibility of life will be entirely bounded, entirely overcome.

Simmel feels that he knows the truth of social and cultural reality. Life is actually imprisoned. Hence, what should be the cause of hope easily edges over into a cause for despair. This is perhaps one of the central messages which is communicated by Georg Simmel's work on the social and the cultural effects of money. In Simmel's interpretation, the money-based economy, and the use of money as a symbol of value, has its home in the modern metropolis. The impact of money, just like the impact of the metropolis itself, on what exists prior to it is quite revolutionary. According to Simmel, 'Money is concerned with what is common to all: it asks for the exchange value, it reduces all quality and individuality to the question: How much?' (Simmel 1950: 411). In other words, money has the effect of establishing form over life.

Money is understood by Simmel to be both a product and a representation of social activity in complex urban societies which are characterized by a division of labour. Money emerges out of a need to oil the wheels of life and exchange in the city, but instead of being a simple means, money emerges as something like an independent end. Instead of widening the milieu of life it actually narrows down boundaries quite dramatically. As such, money is a rational form which not only bounds life but which indeed goes so far as to imprison life by attempting to define it (the knowing of the price of everything and the value of nothing, to paraphrase Oscar Wilde). Consequently a conflict appears. 'All intimate emotional relations between persons are founded in their individuality, whereas in rational relations man is reckoned with like a number, like an element which is itself indifferent. Only the objective measurable achievement is of interest' (Simmel 1950: 411).

Moreover, Simmel evidently could see little or no realistic reason to hope for a transcendence of those restricted and restricting boundaries. It would rather seem that in the face of the money economy, Simmel's dialectical hope was somewhat called into question. After all, money constitutes a web of objectivity. It is involved in every urban, modern exchange relationship. Consequently therefore, the emotional or moral bonds are left virtually nowhere. Money as a system stands above the urbanized human and individual; it confronts her or him as a reality in itself. Indeed, 'since money measures all objects with merciless objectivity, and since its standard of value so measured determines their relationship, a web of objective and personal aspects of life emerges which is similar to the natural cosmos' (Simmel 1990: 431). That similarity resides in the fact that both money and the cosmos are perceived and understood as being entirely cohesive and continuous milieux. Moreover, for Simmel both money and the cosmos are similarly understood as obeying the laws of causality.

With his study of money, Simmel is making and illustrating the point that the boundaries which locate the societal and which give it some kind of direction, can be established and reified to such an extent that they cease to be the framework of human and social freedom. Instead, they come to possess the kinds of properties which are more usually associated with natural forces. They restrict freedom by restricting life and by defining its nature. Consequently, 'The individual has become a mere cog in an enormous organization.' This organization, which encompasses the money economy, the city, the division of labour (that is, this organization which encompasses all those things which reduce life to questions of objective calculation), puts beyond the boundaries of the societal and the cultural 'all progress, spirituality, and value in order to transform them from their subjective form into the form of the purely objective life' (Simmel 1950: 422). In many ways, Lukács's analysis of reification can be read as an echo of themes from Simmel deflected through Marx. However, for Lukács's own, fairly mean, assessment of the significance of Georg Simmel, see Lukács 1991.

Now, Georg Simmel's reflection on the conflict in modern culture is profound and, in many ways, brilliant. It is interesting and demands scrutiny on its own terms. However, what is perhaps even more interesting is the extent to which the story told by Georg Simmel is so deeply insinuated in the consciousness of the modern. It might even be said that with Simmel, it is possible to find one of the clearest expressions of one of the most important myths of European modernity. Stories which have very similar narratives to that told by Simmel pepper modernity (although this is not to deny certain very profound ontological and moral differences. The stories are very different at the deeper epistemological levels, but as simple narratives and as myths they do betray major similarities. As myths of modernity they say comparable things). Karl Marx's discussion of the fetish character of the commodity in capitalist relations of production can be read as a reflection on the ability of ossified cultural forms to become defining of existence and independent of it (Marx 1938). A somewhat less than entirely hopeful version of the myth-story can also be found in Edmund Husserl's important 'Vienna Lecture'.

According to Edmund Husserl, the European spirit was in a deep crisis by the middle of the 1930s. The crisis was a result of the development and establishment of naturalistic science. That science had drawn a sharp distinction between the natural, which was subjected to technical, objective methods of enquiry, and the subjectively meaningful life-world which was simply pushed off the agenda of those things which could be known. In other words, Husserl is approaching the argument that the investigation of the forms of nature was carried out at the expense of a recognition of life itself. Husserl saw himself as trying to reveal the falsity of the disjuncture between the objective *out there* and the subjective *in here*. Husserl wanted to 'show how it happens that the "modern age", which has been so proud for centuries of its theoretical and practical successes, finally becomes involved in a growing dissatisfaction, indeed must view its situation as one of distress' (Husserl 1970: 294).

The deep distress was attributed by Husserl to the fact that: 'Someone who is raised on natural science takes it for granted that everything merely subjective must be excluded and that the natural-scientific method, exhibiting itself in subjective manners of representation, determines objectively' (Husserl 1970: 295). As such, the life-world has become insignificant; science carries on without reference to its subjectivity and instead, talks about it only in so far as it can be objectified and defined within boundaries: 'Since the intuitively given surrounding world, this merely subjective realm, is forgotten in scientific investigation, the working subject is himself forgotten; the scientist does not become a subject of investigation' (Husserl 1970: 295. Arguably this sentence can also be applied to the tendency of much legislative sociology to forget the sociologist. For example, the work of Talcott Parsons might be seen as a prime instance of the problems and difficulties which Husserl thought were produced by objectivity). For Edmund Husserl, the spirit of Europe could only be rescued from the terrible consequences of its forgetting if philosophy reconfirmed the vitality and significance of the life-world. In many ways then, Husserl's phenomenological philosophy was part of a moral programme to help life transcend its natural-scientific, objective boundaries. Husserl was trying to make the case for the recovery of life as subjectivity from the objectified ossification of reification.

The themes and fears of Edmund Husserl also run through the very different, and yet ultimately morally extremely similar, inquiries of Milan Kundera (once again I should stress that I am aware that this leap from Husserl to Kundera might be illicit on epistemological and ontological grounds, but it does seem to be sustainable if the stories they tell are treated as statements and reflections of the myths of modernity). Kundera has discussed Husserl's position and identified his own novels in terms of it. However, whereas Husserl pinned whatever optimism he had on the abilities of phenomenological philosophy to recapture the transcendence of the life-world, and perhaps whereas Simmel pinned his hopes on the demystifying potential of sociological inquiry, Milan Kundera rather unsurprisingly turns to the novel. But not any novel. Only the book which is sympathetic to the 'depreciated legacy of Cervantes' will do (Kundera 1988).

Cervantes is seen by Kundera as almost approaching the status of being the midwife of the modern. The point is that for Cervantes' hero Don Quixote, the world no longer makes complete and self-evident sense. The certainties which had been lent by the form and the figure of God have collapsed. Life is experienced as something without necessary direction or meaning. 'Don Quixote set forth from his house into a world he could no longer recognize.' For Don Quixote, who was riding out to wherever without the guiding hand of God, 'the world suddenly appeared in its fearsome ambiguity; the single divine Truth decomposed into myriad relative truths parcelled out by men' (Kundera 1988: 6).

In other words, through his novel, Cervantes was writing of a world and of an existence in the world which had, or which at least promised to, completely transcend form. The novel went simply where it went; no form such as time could bound the content of the novel and thus give it direction. As Kundera points out, 'The early European novels are journeys through an apparently unlimited world' (Kundera 1988: 7–8).

Consequently according to Kundera, the novel was born out of a reflection on the ambiguity of the world and it contains what might be called 'the wisdom of uncertainty' (Kundera 1988: 7). A novel like *Don Quixote* tells of transcendent life. The book is a challenge to, and an overcoming of all fixed boundaries. It is a testimony for life. Indeed, Kundera seems to equate the legacy of the mode of inquiry which is contained in novels like *Don Quixote* with precisely the life-world which Edmund Husserl tried to rescue by a rather different strategy.

However, Milan Kundera's discussion of the state of the novel is not wildly optimistic. Like Simmel, and more directly like Edmund Husserl, Kundera is also aware that as soon as boundaries are established (and of course, boundaries have to be established to make life make sense), the challenges of life, or of the life-world, or of the Cervantian legacy of ambiguity are hemmed in. Kundera uses literature to trace a history of this process of the increasing restriction of the unlimited possibilities which were faced at the dawn of the modern by Don Quixote. Cervantes' hero could largely go where he wanted and make of the world what he wanted. Similar possibilities lay before the heroes of Diderot's novel *Jacques le Fataliste*. But as the form of the novel and more widely the forms which establish meaning and bound life, take a hold, the unlimited horizons are narrowed down. As such, in the novels of Balzac, 'the distant horizon has disappeared like a landscape behind those modern structures, the social institutions: the police, the law, the world of money and crime, the army, the State' (Kundera 1988: 8). Whereas Don Quixote's world simply went along without purpose, Balzac's is a world where time has been reinterpreted as History. Form has been imposed upon time to make it meaningful.

After Balzac, later in the nineteenth century, and most poignantly for Flaubert's Emma Bovary, the once unbounded horizons have shrunk so much that no escape seems possible except through dreams or death. But at least some escape route is offered. With Emma Bovary, as understood according to Milan Kundera, 'The lost infinity of the outside world is replaced by the infinity of the soul' (Kundera 1988: 8). And by the time of Kafka, even the soul has lost its boundlessness; even personal hopes and ambitions have been pulled into the train of History. For a hero written by Kafka, 'the situation's trap is too terrible, and like a vacuum cleaner it sucks up all his thoughts and feelings, all he can think of is his trial, his surveying job' (Kundera 1988:9). Indeed, in the story *Metamorphosis*, the most frightening consequence of waking up to find oneself turned into a giant beetle is the possibility of arriving late at the office (and in the story, the demolition of humanity becomes a comic incident). In the novels and stories of Franz Kafka, 'The infinity of the soul – if it ever existed – has become a nearly useless appendage' (Kundera 1988: 9). Whereas Don Quixote set out to define adventure for himself and thus to make the world for himself, Kafka's desolate and rather unlikeable characters have the meaning of adventure defined for them. Their lives are wholly bounded by ossified forms which are apprehended as existing of their own accord, quite independently of social or cultural interference.

But in revealing this imprisonment, Milan Kundera is hoping to play at least some part in transcending it. It does not seem to be too inappropriate to suggest that Milan Kundera would enthusiastically agree with Georg Simmel's claim that 'all these sources of form are restraints on life, which wishes to flow creatively from within itself' (Simmel 1971: 381). The recovery of Cervantes is, for Kundera, one way in which the creative wishes of life might be granted.

The point seems to be, then, that the narrative of a conflict in culture between form and life, a conflict which might be understood in terms of a dichotomy between reification and reflexivity, is one of the most popular stories of modernity. I have simply mentioned a couple of especially interesting instances of it. The kind of conflict identified in their different ways, but ultimately for the same ends, by Georg Simmel, Edmund Husserl, Milan Kundera (and of course, Karl Marx, Lukács, Adorno and Horkheimer . . .), is one of the main narratives by which modern relationships and activities go on.

Modernity is understood as progressing in so far as it transcends the products of its own transcendence. The cautionary notes, however, seem to suggest that as modernity becomes its own form (that is, as modernity increasingly becomes the condition for the transcendence of itself), the chances of an escape from ossified reification are held to diminish. Hence the joyous reveries of Don Quixote turn into the petty-minded concerns of the inhabitants of Yonville and later the fears of the peasants in the village beneath the Castle; hence the wonders of Greek philosophy turn into the forgetting of the spirit; hence money becomes something valuable in itself and not simply a medium of exchange, useless in itself. It would seem that one of the main worries of those who reflect upon the requirements and the basis of their modernity is precisely the fear that they might not be able to overcome the conditions of their own modernity. It might be said that to some extent Simmel and the others are thrashing against the possibility that they might be written by Kafka rather than written by Diderot or Cervantes.

Certainly these myths and worries can be found in Max Weber's essay

'Science as a Vocation'. Indeed, the essay provides an especially clear statement of the conflicts of modernity precisely because Weber was trying to develop a case which was at once compatible with the concern to make meaning in the world through the identification of boundaries and yet which could also maintain a commitment to the transcendence of boundaries. As such, and for these purposes, perhaps the most important part of the essay is the moment when Weber declares that science is an activity which necessarily makes its achievements redundant and out of date. As Weber said, 'Every scientific "fulfilment" raises new "questions"; it asks to be "surpassed" and out-dated. Whoever wishes to serve science has to resign himself to this fact' (Weber 1948: 138). In other words, Weber is suggesting that the very meaning of science is the deliberate transcendence of the boundaries of science: 'Scientific works . . . will be surpassed scientifically – let that be repeated – for it is our common fate and, more, our common goal. We cannot work without hoping that others will advance further than we have' (Weber 1948: 138).

Now Weber is making a number of interesting claims here. They illustrate not only Simmel's conflict in modern culture, but they also go rather a long way towards revealing the myth of modernity. Most obviously, Weber is making a very powerful and important demand for the transcendence of ossified scientific form and thus, for the ability of social and cultural activity to be defining of itself. To this extent then, the purpose of science is to render the achievements of all previous science obsolete. But Weber's case is based on some rather more implicit suppositions. The point is that, for Weber, science is to be transcended by science and moreover, that through that self-overcoming, science is to continue. In other words, behind the strong appeal for the overcoming of boundaries, Max Weber simply has to presuppose the reification of a form of inquiry and knowledge which is called, and which will be called, science. The form and the identity of science is taken as fixed when the activity of science is, by contrast, taken as fluid.

In the 'Science as a Vocation' essay Max Weber assumes, and simply takes entirely for granted, the historical continuity from past, through the present and into the future, of a bounded and identifiable enterprise. Weber's argument only really makes sense if what Newton, for example, did yesterday and Einstein does today, stand in some line of direct descent with what physicists will do tomorrow. For all of the practitioners, and for all time, the meanings and the requirements of science, the activities and methods which constitute science, must be self-evident and emphatically not transcended. The bounded horizons of that which is science must never be overcome, else science could not continue; it could not throw all the previous achievements of science onto the scrap-heap (not least because previous achievements could not necessarily be identified as science). So, in order for modernity to go on (or at least, in order for modernity to go on in accordance with the requirements of the mythical narrative of modernity), some of the products of modernity must be taken as existing in perpetuity.

As such, there is a rather profound contradiction in Weber's essay. The contradiction is social and cultural rather than a simple failure of nerve or intelligence on the part of Max Weber himself. Either all boundaries are transcended and science loses all direction and purpose (it quite literally becomes pointless), or some boundaries are never transcended and thus, the meanings of science are restricted. Science can talk about everything except the legitimacy of science (this possibility was, of course, one of the main causes for the concerns of Edmund Husserl). Science can develop no concept of science (although there can be lengthy, tedious, and fruitless debates about what science is given that science takes place). Either way, the institutions and arrangements of modernity were thus consigned to perpetual inadequacy from the point of view of the myth of modernity. They are preconditions of transcendence which, however, cannot be transcended themselves.

Thanks to the reflections and worries of those individuals who sought to understand their existence (and I have of course highlighted some of the efforts of just a very few of them), it is possible to see that existence was understood (by those who set about the enterprise of understanding) in terms of involvement in a milieu of conflict. On the one hand, the emergence and consolidation of bounded forms were identified as the only way in which life could be given direction, meaning and location. Only through the establishment of forms was it possible to identify some horizons in the otherwise limitless and sublime world. These forms required some definition of life and indeed, the pushing of life into bounded spheres. But, on the other hand, life was apprehended in one guise or another as an almost mythical force which sought to overcome any boundaries which were imposed upon its freedom to roam throughout the world. Life was understood as being self-sufficient and defining of itself.

Consequently, the narratives which embodied these contradictions tended to fall into one or another of three categories. Firstly, the narratives could make appeals for, or at least represent without judgement, the limitation of the horizons of life by boundaries. To some extent, this narrative can be located in the work of Durkheim. Secondly, and in opposition to the first category, the narratives could represent a demand for the wholesale transcendence of boundaries. This narrative strategy can be seen in the work of Nietzsche. Thirdly, and in the most subtle hands, the narratives could be brought together into a dialectical synthesis which, however, emphasized a unity in conflict. The most careful thinkers were able to realize that the hermeneutic need for boundaries went hand in hand with a desire to transcend those boundaries. The likes of Simmel (and in a different way Sigmund Freud) knew that without boundaries no boundaries could be transcended, that the sense of reification was the precondition for the sense of reflexivity.

As such, what Simmel called the modern culture, or what Husserl and then Milan Kundera called Europe, was by no means a monolith. It was understood, explained, and felt differently from one social and cultural position to another. Similarly, the meaning of existence in the world, and the answer to the perceived problems of that existence, varied dramatically depending on the attitude which was adopted to each of the different narrative possibilities. Now, although this interpretation of the problems and possibilities associated with boundaries is very useful if not (in the right hands; not my hands) potentially profound, it does contain a difficulty. Basically, the usefulness of Simmel, Husserl, Kundera and so forth can be demonstrated fairly easily in so far as they show the fractured nature of culture. But their analyses operate in terms of a philosophy of history and certain ontological categories which perhaps should not be left unchallenged.

In particular, the concept of life as it is used by Georg Simmel warrants a little investigation. Some time should be spent exploring precisely what this force is which is said to involve the transcendence of boundaries. But Simmel denied that the meaning of life could actually be explored and even less the meaning of life be said. The problem is fairly obvious; if life is transcendent in relation to form, then to say what life involves is to establish a form of life and thus, to do violence to it. Simmel acknowledged this problem in the footnote to the 'Conflict in Modern Culture' essay. He showed the bounds of his own interpretation of culture when he wrote that 'Since life is the antithesis of form, and since that which is somehow formed can be conceptually described, the concept of life cannot be freed from logical imprecision'. The implication is obvious: 'The essence of life would be denied if one tried to form an exhaustive conceptual definition' (Simmel 1971: 392). In other words, and a little like Husserl's life-world, Simmel's category of life is actually prior to and incompatible with any objective statement or understanding. It can only be intuited or spoken of in the most vague terms because to speak with clarity would be to impose illicit boundaries on that which is necessarily without bounds.

Not to put too fine a point on the matter, this is a mystification. Because Simmel cannot say what life is, neither can he take the much vaunted argument about the transcendence of form by life very much further than a simple assertion. But Simmel's analysis of the nature of the conflict in modern culture deserves better than that. Perhaps this aporia in Simmel's thought can be avoided if his reflections are disentangled from a philosophy of history and instead, put into a far more explicitly sociological context. It might then be possible to say what this category of life actually involves; what makes it up and where it comes from. Similarly, the tendencies towards the reification of boundaries would then be a fully social and cultural process (as, indeed, Simmel more than implied in his reflection on the philosophy of money). To this extent, I wish to propose that the nature of the conflict which Simmel and the others quite accurately identified in modern culture, is to be understood as an expression of a conflict between what might be called a *will to certainty* and a *will to know*.

The use of the word 'will' should be clarified. I am not using the word in any sense after Schopenhauer or Nietzsche. I am simply trying to imply a kind of hermeneutic determination to make the things of the world make sense. In these terms, that purpose to understand can be achieved through two paradigmatic strategies. Either meaning can be established through the identification of criteria of truth which allow for certainty, or meaning can be established through the identification of the basis upon which it is possible to know. The point to note is that these strategies are fundamentally irreconcilable with each other and importantly, they are both socially and culturally contingent. They only exist in certain social and cultural circumstances, and they only try to meet social and cultural hermeneutic needs. There is nothing mysterious or essential about either of them. In particular, they only emerge in the wake of the deconstruction of natural artifice.

According to the useful discussion provided by Agnes Heller, the term 'natural artifice' can be applied to the pre-modern hermeneutic strategies, and it might be added the boundary construction practices, which imply that social and cultural arrangements are arranged by nature (Heller 1990: 145). In other words, within the condition dominated by natural artifice, the world is understood as being simply the way it has to be. And it has to be the way it is because of the command of some authority who is beyond the boundaries of social and cultural interference. The obvious example of such an authority is, of course, God. According to Heller, the commitment to such arrangement by nature can be understood as the defining trait of the pre-modern. However, the condition of modernity is ushered in at the moment when the arrangements which were previously understood as nature are, instead, understood as the product of human artifice. As Agnes Heller explains, 'What is natural to the pre-modern conception is no longer natural to the modern one. Modern imagination begins to emerge when and where the "natural" appears as artificial; a man-made construct that can be deconstructed' (Heller 1990: 145). Indeed, the very awareness of the essential artificiality of all previous boundaries which were justified by reference to nature is in itself a deconstruction of the pre-modern forms.

It is precisely such a condition of modernity which the story of Don Quixote reflects. Cervantes' hero rode out into a world in which the boundaries which had once seemed to be natural (because coherent, continuous and seamless) no longer necessarily held good. Instead, Don Quixote went out into a world which he experienced as it were in the seams. Therefore the world of Don Quixote was an adventure in ambivalence. It was also a classic moment in the ability of social and cultural institutions and arrangements to be self-sufficiently self-defining (so that, for example, a grubby inn becomes a glittering castle). However, and if Milan Kundera is right (and even if he is not, the suggestion is extremely stimulating), the history of the European novel might be interpreted as the history of the bounding of Don Quixote. Don Quixote is a founding figure of the modern imagination because he knows that the natural is in fact artificial. But Josef K. in *The Trial*, and perhaps even more the Land Surveyor in *The Castle*, are trapped within the continuous boundaries of modernity because what was once artificial is now understood as if it were a blind natural force like the cosmos.

But of course, there is a problem. If modernity meant a deconstruction of natural artifice (if indeed modernity initially represented the revelation of the contingent and fabricated status of the seemingly inevitable natural boundaries), then the expressions and protagonists of the modern condition were confronted with the problems of making the world make sense and of giving the human a place and a direction in it. After all, modernity cannot know itself by reference to nature (and neither, therefore, can it know itself by reference to God). The modern condition can only be known by reference to itself. Within the modern condition, the world is made to make sense through the identification and establishment of boundaries which are either known through appeals to rather reified standards of certainty or through appeals to more reflexive enterprises of self-knowledge.

In other words, whilst both the pre-modern and the modern conditions base hermeneutic and existential meaning, location and direction on boundaries, the justifications of those boundaries are necessarily different from the one condition to the other. Whereas pre-modern boundaries referred to something which was beyond, the modern boundaries refer to something within. But the modern reference could be of one of two contradictory kinds. The struggle for certainty over the meaning of things, which I am calling the will to certainty, is in many ways dealing with the same issues as Georg Simmel's forms. It involves the establishment of ossifications which are understood as tending to take on an independent existence and which, therefore, attempt to say something definite and certain about existence by fixing its meanings. Meanwhile, the struggle to know of the meaning of the world, which I am calling the will to know, is in many ways dealing with the same issues as Georg Simmel's life (albeit in a rather different way). It involves an attempt to understand and explain (and therefore implicitly transcend) the ossification and reification of boundaries.

The will to certainty more or less inevitably implies the establishment and identification of boundaries which are themselves understood to be beyond question. After all, the will to certainty means nothing other than the attempt to transform the 'infinite spaces of our worlds', an infinity and potential plurality which is the consequence of the deconstruction of natural artifice, into a singularity with direction. The will to certainty involves projects of the location of things by reference to a single, socially and culturally identified Truth. Simply, it means fixed identities. The boundaries themselves are the precondition for certainty and therefore, they are themselves incontestable. In order for the world to be bounded and made to make sense as either a society, or a teleological process or whatever, the boundaries have to be taken for granted. The boundaries have to come to stand apart from the social and the cultural activities which were framed by them.

Of course, these moves can be seen in Weber's thoughts on science, but they can be found in other important statements of modernity as well. Perhaps Immanuel Kant's essay 'What is Enlightenment?' can be interpreted as one example of the tendency of the will to certainty to involve reification. It is quite clear from the essay that whilst Kant can define Enlightenment as something which gives a direction to change, he is actually unable to found the case for Enlightenment as anything more than an assertion. The notion of Enlightenment is the precondition for Kant's statement of the case for Enlightenment and therefore, the desirability of Enlightenment is simply taken for granted. In a way which anticipates Max Weber's comments on science, Kant's essay is quite incapable of developing any concept of Enlightenment since the assumption of Enlightenment is the unsayable predicate of the essay. Kant uses the assumed authority of Enlightenment, and therefore the taken for granted certainty lent by a process, to replace the certainties which had been established and assumed when God was the sovereign authority. As such, Enlightenment itself is reified, it is a boundary which comes to be interpreted as something apart. It is a movement which turns individuals into cogs. All of this is despite the fact that Enlightenment as Kant brilliantly understood it nevertheless required resolute individual action (see Kant 1970).

The will to know is rather more interesting. It does not involve the replacement of one reference and identity of certainty with another. Quite the opposite, the will to know actually implies the deconstruction of all certainty in the name of the ability of the social and the cultural to reveal artifice and thus define for itself its own place and direction in the world. In other words, whereas the will to certainty implies a universalization of a single set of boundaries, the will to know implies the multiplication of particular boundaries. The will to know, which is typically manifest in interpretive social and cultural studies, and following Kundera in the literature which applauds Cervantes, seeks to make the world intelligible by revealing the status of the taken for granted certainties. So, for example, Marx and Engels sought to know the truth of Kant's utterances about Enlightenment and consequently revealed the assumptions of Kant to be the product and the expression of contingent relationships (Marx and Engels 1970). Essentially then, the will to know involves an attempt to see the existing reifications (that is, the existing forms) as things to be interrogated and interpreted rather than simply taken for granted. No certainty is to be simply and unreflexively accepted.

The will to know is, in a nutshell, transcendent in relation to the products of the will to certainty. The two wills, which are both ex-pressions of the hermeneutic difficulties which emerge in the wake of the deconstruction of natural artifice, stand in a dialectical relationship of antagonism towards one another.

So far, this is all very reminiscent of Georg Simmel. So far, I have actually done little more than restate with new jargon the argument that life is transcendent in relation to form, but that the forms can take on a reality of their own which is interpreted as imprisoning from the point of view of life. The point is, however, that it is not too useful to see what Simmel calls life as some spiritual or inherently indefinable energy. Rather, the pressures and interests which Simmel was seeking to explain are, perhaps, best seen as the product of solely social and cultural forces. In particular, I wish to propose that what Simmel calls life is better explained in terms of the expressions of a particular position within a culture of reflexive discourse (I am using the phrase 'culture of reflexive discourse' after Alvin Gouldner; see Gouldner 1975, 1985).

The culture of reflexive discourse arises out of the ability of specific social groups to engage in practices of the deconstruction and revelation of the artificiality of anything which is understood as existing by nature. To this extent then it is justifiable to say that the culture is an expression of the activity and interests of groupings within the community of the intellectuals. Through it, these critical, reflexive intellectuals are able to express whatever shared community they might have and are, moreover, able to make claims to be the vanguard of social and cultural self-definition precisely because they wish to know rather than wish to be certain. Basically, the activities of the reflexive intellectuals entail a refusal to accept any boundaries as things which simply must be taken for granted. Their activities also entail a refusal to necessarily accept the references to certain truth which are made by others. As such, the reflexive intellectuals are about nothing other than the overcoming of all existing ossifications and forms.

As Alvin Gouldner wrote, 'The intellectuals' culture of careful and critical discourse implies that it is now possible for anyone, however rich and powerful, to speak wrongly' (Gouldner 1975: 20). Through their discursive and hermeneutic commitments, then, these intellectuals seek to read off statements of certainty against the social position of the speaker (exactly the line of attack which Marx and Engels launched against Kant). In so doing, the certainty is undermined and shown to be possibly embedded in self-interest. The reflexive intellectuals are characterized by a will to know the social determination of certainty. Consequently they will to undermine everything which is contained within self-evident bounds. From their point of view all boundaries are actually or potentially open to doubt: 'whatever is *may* be wrong or may be made better. What exists is now subject to negation, to critique, and to judgment' (Gouldner 1975: 20). The implication is obvious (or at least, thanks to Alvin Gouldner the implication of the culture of reflexive discourse is obvious). It implies 'a politically revolutionizing potential that *rejects* the conventional political and economic institutions' (Gouldner 1975: 21). As Alvin Gouldner says in the specific case of intellectuals as scholars: 'Searching out and transcending the conventional boundaries of "normal" scholarship, they are an irritant to conventional scholars, who condemn them as deviants. Rather than operating safely within the familiar boundaries of an established paradigm, intellectuals violate boundaries' (Gouldner 1975: 23).

So, intellectuals seek to know the nature and the implications of boundaries. According to the useful distinction drawn by Gouldner, the situation is rather different for what he terms the technical intelligentsia. Certainly, these technicians are implicated in the culture of reflexive discourse (they too are seeking to understand the modern by referring it solely to itself, without reference to some outside authority). But, as Gouldner says, in a passage which is explicitly drawing on the insights and vocabulary of Thomas Kuhn, 'The technician. . .accepts the dominant paradigm in his field; he operates within it, pursuing its implications, applying its general principles to new fields; but he does not focalize or criticize the boundaries of the paradigm itself' (Gouldner 1975: 23).

In these terms then, and to exaggerate a little for the sake of illustration, it might be said that the Immanuel Kant of the Enlightenment essay, and the Max Weber of the 'Science as a Vocation' piece, are both members of the technical intelligentsia. They share a similar concern to work within the boundaries of a certainty and thus fail, or simply do not want, to interrogate the basis of their taken for granted principles. Put another way, the technical intelligentsia operate in terms of the culture of reflexive discourse but in a way which emphasizes certainty. The intelligentsia operate within boundaries, whereas the intellectuals try to move without boundaries. To quote Gouldner once again, 'The intelligentsia are thus harvesters, not planters, from the point of view of intellectuals.' For the technical intelligentsia, 'The question here is "fruitfulness;" but the "tree" bearing the fruit is regarded as in being' (Gouldner 1975: 24).

The transcendence of the reified forms does not have to be attributed to some almost mystical force called life. Indeed, neither is it the case that the nature of the transcending force cannot be said (as Simmel of course argued was the case with life). Rather, the will to transcend established forms, that is the dialectical conflict between the tendency towards reification and the tendency towards reflexivity, can be understood in sociological terms alone. Indeed, the conflict itself is derived out of a sociological and hermeneutic disagreement over the meaningfulness of the world and the place of things in the world in the wake of deconstruction of natural artifice. There is nothing unsayable about any of this at all.

If the conflict between reification and reflexivity is seen in sociological-hermeneutic terms, then it is also the case that it becomes very obvious that the conflict in modern culture is itself variable and negotiable in its playing out. For example, both Kant and Weber were able to move from the community of the intelligentsia to the community of the intellectuals with no great difficulty; perhaps that movement was a product of the ambivalent status of their reflexive interests and activities. But nuclear physicists tend not to move from the one pole to the other except in moments of profound crisis (for example Robert Oppenheimer). Simply, whilst it might well be the case that reified forms (that is, the necessary boundaries) are understood as imprisoning, such an understanding is only possible from the point of view of the intellectuals of the culture of reflexive discourse.

The conflict in modern culture is something which is felt most keenly by reflexive intellectuals since it is they who are most deeply committed to the enterprise of deconstruction. Only the specific groups of reflexive intellectuals typically want to know; all other social groups, typically such as the technical intelligentsia, simply ask (or are made to ask) for certainty in the world and in their existence. Boundaries are only restraints from the perspective informed and established by one attitude within the culture of reflexive discourse; boundaries are not necessarily understood as a restraint from every social and cultural site.

I want to propose two theses. Firstly, reflexivity is transcendent in relation to reification. Secondly, reflexivity is the intimation of boundlessness. This intimation of boundlessness is not, therefore, necessarily boundlessness as such (it is merely a tendency to look towards boundlessness), and neither is it a universal and a homogeneous cultural movement. The intimation of boundlessness is an expression of the perspective on the world which is typical and characteristic of the intellectuals. (To clarify the use of this word: I am not implying that intellectuals are only found in certain faculties on the University campus. Following Gramsci to some extent, and following him for my own purposes, it is at least potentially true that everyone can be an intellectual in so far as, thanks to modernity, everyone is in one way or another potentially involved in the culture of reflexive discourse.) Those groups or activities which do not have some involvement in the culture of reflexive discourse, or which rather more importantly adopt a technical attitude towards its deconstructive effects, will not be transcendent in relation to reified forms and neither, therefore, will their conditions of existence be an intimation of boundlessness. Quite probably, they will not apprehend the boundaries as prisons; rather the boundaries are more likely to be apprehended as so many possibilities.

The notion of the intimation of a world without bounds is one very useful way of coming to terms with the status and meaning of the debates on post-modernity. Post-modernity is not an era which can be dated and neither is it an entirely new cultural and hermeneutic configuration. Rather, post-modernity is nothing other than a perspective on modernity which is itself dependent on modernity. Post-modernity can be interpreted as the condition of the intimation of boundlessness, but that intimation is only possible because it is established on the basis of the modern boundaries. It is a condition without the boundaries of what are held to be the ossified and reified modern forms.

As Agnes Heller and Ferenc Fehér have written (although for different reasons), 'postmodernity may be understood as the private-collective time and space, within the wider time and space of modernity, delineated by those who have problems with and queries addressed to modernity' (Heller and Fehér 1988: 1). So post-modernity is a condition which only makes sense to the extent that it is considered in relationship with the modern. As such: 'Those who have chosen to dwell in post-modernity nevertheless live among moderns as well as premoderns. For the very foundation of postmodernity consists of viewing the world as a plurality of heterogeneous spaces and temporalities' (Heller and Fehér 1988: 1). Post-modernity is a condition which is dependent on the modern. It represents the hermeneutic conflict in modernity as it is seen from the point of view of the intellectuals who are committed to the claims of the culture of reflexive discourse. It is only from that space and time that modernity is seen as a series of reifications which need to be, and indeed, can be, transcended.

Post-modernity is the intimation from within modernity of a condition without bounds of modernity. What this means in more concrete terms, of course, is that from the point of view of the certain modern boundaries, post-modernity seems to be directionless, blurred and lacking in rigour. But from the point of view of post-modernity, modernity with its boundaries is a prison of one sort or another towards which the only proper attitude is one of incredulity.

It is for these reasons that I have chosen to talk about *post-modernity* rather than *postmodernity*. There is more at stake here than a hyphen. The difficulty with *postmodernity* as anything more than a convenient label is that it implies a clear distinction between it and the modern. Post-modernity has resonances of the kind of sharp break between epochs or states of consciousness which the kind of argument I have proposed seeks to deny. Basically, I am saying that it is at best trivial and at worst completely futile to find the morning or afternoon when the world entered into postmodernity. However, *post-modernity* implies a more complex series of connections. Indeed, the status of post-modernity as a primarily *intimated* condition adds to that complexity. It implies that the post-modern is not distinctly different but that, rather, it can only exist in relation with the modern. The post-modern and the modern are not divisible; they go together.

Chapter 2

Identity

If, from the point of view of modernity, the pre-modern milieu is interpreted as dominated and defined by the rigours and restrictions of natural artifice, then modernity initially appears to itself as an artificial, deliberately constructed world (and therefore the history of modernity becomes one of a story of the forgetting of the artificiality). In other words, in relation to the natural or God-given house for humanity which is held to prevail in the pre-modern condition, the house for humanity which is constructed in the relationships and processes of modernity is, so to speak, a fabricated dwelling.

Consequently, and as an extension of all of this, if it can be said that to live in the modern world is to live in a world which has had to be purposefully fabricated after the wreckage of natural artifice (and to the extent that the modern world emerges out of a deconstruction of the taken for granted, it is possible to say just that), then it is also possible to say that two attitudes can be taken towards the dwelling of the human and of meaning which is constructed in the relationships of modernity to replace the defining and time-honoured edifice which went before.

The new modern dwelling can be accepted as the warm and comforting cradle of certainty and confidence. In that case, great efforts will be taken to improve on the architecture bequeathed by the parents to their children. Great efforts will be taken to forget the possibly shaky foundations of the house and, instead, no expenditure will be spared on the improvement of the wall-paper and the ornamentation (the abyss outside the front door will be hidden). No price will be too much for the latest technological advances which will increase the value of the home for the present inhabitants and, it is hoped, the future generations. The house itself will become a place to be taken for granted. It will become the legacy which proves beyond doubt the genius of the builder. When the cracks appear in the walls the house will not be demolished. Instead a little bit of cosmetic surgery will be carried out. The cracks will be hidden or, in more dire cases, bound together by iron. In any case, the inhabitants will probably be unable to hear the falling masonry because they will be too busy listening to their wonderful new hi-fi systems or revelling in the beauty of the latest dishwasher. The modern order of things will take on an air of permanence and longevity to the extent that it is left unchallenged by those it shelters.

Alternatively, however, it is possible that some of the children will look to the building of the parents and, instead of accepting it as a gift and as a haven in a stormy world, they will try to have a look at the foundations. The house will not be taken for granted as the inevitable and only possible sturdy dwelling. Rather it will be approached with pickaxes and drills as the children try to find out how the parents did what they did, as the children try to discover if the house will be sturdy enough for the wild parties which are planned. But as soon as a pickaxe reveals a foundation, as soon as the foundation is known to be safe and sturdy, it is opened up to the elements. It is, in fact, ruined. The walls will come tumbling down at the exact moment when the guests arrive and when the music is turned to full volume.

To be certain about the dwelling is to be confined within its walls and to let the walls define and determine what might be done. The dominant attitude towards it is one of an entirely bounded technical strategy of the improvement of what is already given. But to know the dwelling is quite possibly to undermine it; to know is to transgress the boundaries of certainty. Most definitely, to know the dwelling is to intimate a time when it might no longer exist. To want to know is to intimate a condition in which the old house has become either the deeply buried ancestor of the new one (here, think of Freud's splendid evocation of the layers of Rome at the beginning of *Civilization and its Discontents*), or it has become a place within something quite beyond it (just like the cathedral in Cordoba's mosque). In either case, as soon as the dwelling is known it is to one degree or another transcended.

Similarly, and I hope it is clear that I have been talking metaphorically, the post-modern condition is the intimation of a situation without the boundaries of modernity. Post-modernity is associated with the children who wield the pickaxes rather than with the children who discuss the brilliance of digital audio technology. The contented and happy listeners are inhabiting a condition within the boundaries of the modern forms. Unlike the protagonists of post-modernity, they do not want, do not imagine, do not understand, any transcendence of the existing bounded forms.

But the transcendence is an intimation. It is not necessarily a transcendence as such. In other words, it might well be little more than a style. Consequently, it might well tend to emphasize a play with the ornamentation of the dwelling rather than with the dwelling itself. The juxtaposition of baroque porticos with plastic pillars might well be taken to be tantamount to a demolition of the house when in fact it will merely be a game with the house (and a game at that which the time-honoured and now traditional house is quite likely to win; in a similar vein, Marcel Duchamp's *Bicycle Wheel* reinvigorated art rather than undermined it). It is perhaps intrinsic to the condition of post-modernity that it is difficult to know where, if anywhere, style ends and transcendence begins. It is difficult to know if there is actually anything more to the post-modern than a series of more or less incoherent intimations which might, or then again might not, come to very much.

However, even if the attitude towards the modern reification is in fact little more than stylistic, it is still the case that simple games of ornamentation involve a transformation of its status. The point is that the modern house can be deconstructed to some extent through intimation alone. Whatever the status of the post-modern it is still a transcendence of the given and, therefore, the opening up of new freedoms and new possibilities in the human and the cultural self-definition of the world. But these events which, it might be objected, are specific to the realm of hermeneutic constructions go beyond the intellectual sphere alone. They do indeed have an effect on material practices in the world since they radically transform the identity and the imagined constitution of that world. Moreover, the intimations of boundlessness tend to have wide implications to the extent that they move outside of their originating time and place amongst the community of the intellectuals.

This movement beyond the intellectuals occurs for two reasons. Firstly, in modernity the precise constituency of the intellectuals cannot be pinned down with very great accuracy or ease. Certainly, some social groups might carry out processes of closure and ritual differentiation against all other groups so that they can claim the title of 'intellectuals' for themselves (for example, the kinds of people who read and write books about post-modernity are aware of themselves as 'intellectuals' in some sense), but it is also the case that in principle anyone and everyone who participates in a deconstruction of natural artifice and who tries to transgress the given can to some extent claim the label of 'intellectual' for themselves and their colleagues.

Secondly, to the extent that the intellectuals add their own ornamentation and styles to the modern they are transforming the appearance of the reified fabrication of the order of things. The intellectuals can make things seem to be different from how they were. Thanks to them the dwelling looks different and, therefore, it can no longer be taken entirely for granted ('Should the waste-disposal pipes be on the outside?'). Even the technical intelligentsia who fairly unproblematically live in the house consequently have to be able to direct some attention towards the boundaries even if only to prove that the assumed boundaries are, in fact, still in place and that there is actually nothing to worry about. The dwelling might well emerge stronger from the attempt to subvert it through stylistic manoeuvres, but the victory cannot be relied upon. The victory has to be fought for. The foundation and security of the form of the dwelling has to be known to be safe and secure. Even if only to a modest degree, it ceases to be utterly and self-evidently certain.

As such, the post-modern intimation of the condition without bounds tends to seep outside of the rather narrow community of the self-proclaimed and quite often professionalized intellectuals. It tends to become a pervasive social and cultural issue. It tends to take a place in all the enterprises and activities through which the world is approached as an occasion for, and in terms of the possibility of, the practice of reflexivity (whatever status the reflexivity might have, intellectual, hermeneutic, financial, architectural).

So, Agnes Heller and Ferenc Fehér are making a useful point when they say that post-modernity is a private time and space within the modern (Heller and Fehér 1988: 1). But it should also be appreciated that the extent of that private place tends to grow. It tends to escape and go beyond its own restricted horizons. Yet, and as Georg Simmel always remembered, the escape into the intimation of boundlessness is only possible because there is some bounded place from which escape is interpreted as necessary, desirable or even possible. The boundaries and the boundlessness, and of course this means also the modernity and post-modernity, go together. There has to be something to transgress in the first place; there has to be some boundary which makes transgression a transgression.

The intertwining of form and transcendence, boundaries and boundlessness, is demonstrated very clearly in the history of the attempts to unravel fixed identities in social and cultural relationships. Within the institutions and arrangements of modernity, the unravelling of fixed identities for social and cultural groups, individuals or processes was especially important. If an identity could be fixed and thus supposedly known once and for all, it could also be the basis for certainty. The unravelling of fixed identities makes the world a rather less mysterious place. On the one hand, the identification of fixed identities meant that the world was able to be made to make sense (it was in principle possible to know the supposed secrets of social and cultural relationships since their core was assumed to be stable from time to time and from place to place). But on the other hand the establishment of fixed identities turned them into boundaries which were able to claim a right to force recalcitrant activities and attitudes into their framework or which were interpreted by the intellectuals as things which had to be transcended in the name of freedom.

With this stress on the struggle for freedom, the modern hermeneutic of the world as a bounded place where things had a definite place and a single meaning (that is, the construction of the world as a place of oppression), intimated, or at least contained the germ of its own overcoming. Indeed, given that modernity involved the establishment and the practice of single and irrevocable identities, any transcendence implied a turn to a multiplicity of identities which were interpreted as boundless. But, unsurprisingly, it did not take too long for even those intimations of transcendence to become identified as boundaries and therefore, as forms which themselves needed to be gone beyond.

The endless dialectical history of form–transcendence–form–transcendence (this conflict in modern culture), is illustrated especially clearly in the narratives which expressed and created the identity of the proletariat simultaneously as a class of the here and now and as a revolutionary subject of the not too distant future. Indeed it is especially important and useful to explore the difficult progress of the identity of the proletariat since that class was, in many ways, the great hope of modern freedom. Its fate can be seen as a crystallization of the fate of modernity itself.

The narratives of the proletariat can be read in terms of successive attempts on the part of reflexive interests and intellectuals to make the world move without bounds, even though the bounds they seek to overcome are themselves the products of statements of earlier intimations of boundlessness. With the example of the proletariat it is possible to see that identity is interpreted simultaneously as a precondition for hermeneutic confidence and yet a prison from which escape has to be effected.

The difficult history of class identity, and of course especially proletarian identity, is revealed particularly clearly in the work of Karl Marx. Given the magnificence of Marx's thought, and in view of his profound ability to discover the secrets of modernity, that should not be at all surprising. On the one hand, Marx used the idea of class to make sense of the existing world and the relationships in it. For Marx, this world is interpreted as a giant prison of forms which emerge out of the capitalist relations of production. But on the other hand, Karl Marx was in no doubt that the forms of class and of class-divided society needed to be, could be, and eventually would be transcended so that a presently essentially unsayable universal boundlessness could be intimated (Communism). As such, for Marx the future world was to be a reflexive one which was transcendent in relation to the existent world which was thus rendered as a series of continuous reification. But recent contributions to the debates surrounding class identity and especially the destiny of the Revolutionary Proletariat have revealed a tendency to go beyond the once-but-no-more boundlessness intimated by Marx.

In the otherwise completely different work of, say, André Gorz and Jean Baudrillard, it is nevertheless possible to see a fairly similar move of the deconstruction of the boundlessness intimated by Marx. That deconstruction is justified on the grounds that the old intimations have now become fixed and bounded. In other words, Marx reflexively transcended the forms of capitalist society and people like Gorz and Baudrillard have reflexively transcended (what to them as later reflexive intellectuals are) the forms of Marx's proletariat. Hand in hand with that process of reinterpretation, the status of Marxism and the self-proclaimed Marxists was transformed during the first eighty or ninety years of the twentieth century. To the extent that the self-anointed Marxists were successful in pragmatic and practical terms, they ceased to be intellectuals. Instead they tended to become a technical intelligentsia. They tended to gloat upon their own achievements around the house; they tended to forget about the world outside the front door.

Karl Marx interpreted the present as one of the imprisonment of potentially self-defining humanity within defining and restraining forms. Indeed, Marx implies that the prison is so tight that humanity as a quality of being has been virtually snuffed out (for a valuable discussion of some reasons why Marx saw capitalist society in this light, see Gouldner 1985). In many ways, this is a main part of the story of estrangement which can be found in the *Economic and Philosophic Manuscripts* (Marx 1977). The story which Marx tells is one of the dissolution of humanity and of the dehumanization of the modern (and therefore formally human) world by the ossified products, the forms, of labour. Put another way, in the *Economic and Philosophic Manuscripts*, Karl Marx is telling of the division of the world into objects and subjects. And the tragedy of modernity is precisely that the objects produced by humanity take on a life of their own. Like Simmel's forms they become defining of the human when in fact the human ought to be defining of them.

According to Karl Marx the subjective achievements of the worker ironically reduces the worker to the level of an object. Marx emphasized the contradiction in a passage which almost seems to anticipate Georg Simmel in both language and moral concern (although Georg Simmel was no Marxist of course. In any case I hope it is clear from my argument that the adherence or otherwise to something called Marxism is, hermenuetically, of rather secondary importance when compared to the analysis of modernity). The contradiction between what ought to be and what is was drawn out when Karl Marx wrote that 'In labour all the natural, spiritual, and social variety of individual activity is manifested and is variously rewarded, whilst dead capital always keeps the same pace and is indifferent to *real* individual activity' (Marx 1977: 19).

For Marx, the individual should be self-sufficiently self-defining through labour (and Marx seems to understand labour in much the same vitalist terms as Simmel understood life). But the formal arrangement of labour in capitalist relationships of ownership and production (that is, the current institution of the conditions of possibility of labour) has the effect of bounding individual activity. The forms of capitalist production are ossified and stand apart from the individual; they confront the individual as objects (even though the individual has been objectified by the capitalist arrangements). From the point of view of the creative and living individual, capitalist forms are, in fact, quite dead.

The moral outrage of Marx's work is contained in his proposition that this dead society produces dead inhabitants. Thanks to the requirements of capitalist relationships of production (such as wage labour and profit), the worker ceases to be a living creator of meaning. Instead the worker is the object of meanings which are imposed from outside, through dull compulsion. Marx argued that as the material riches of society increase exponentially, there is a corresponding restriction and finally a complete annihilation of the quality of humanity. 'The *devaluation* of the world of men is in direct proportion to the *increasing value* of the world of things' (Marx 1977: 63). With the capitalist production of things it is possible to identify a process of 'overwork and premature death, decline to a mere machine, a bond servant of capital, which piles up dangerously over and against him, more competition, and starvation or beggary for a section of the workers' (Marx 1977: 21).

The world with its objects becomes something which 'piles up dangerously'. It becomes something which defines meaning, place and identity rather than something through which meaning, place and identity are defining of themselves. Indeed, to buy things like hi-fi systems or dishwashers is not to escape entrapment. The consumption of the goods of capitalism does not buy freedom. Quite the opposite, to the extent that those things are capitalist forms, to consume them is actually to sink even deeper into the prison. Famously, 'the more the worker spends himself, the more powerful becomes the alien world of objects which he creates over and against himself, the poorer he himself – his inner world – becomes, the less belongs to him as his own' (Marx 1977: 63). Marx continued to put the same point rather more precisely: 'The worker puts his life into the object; but now his life no longer belongs to him but to the object' (Marx 1977: 63).

This is, of course, the nub of Marx's account of the alienation of the worker in capitalist relationships of production. Now, it would obviously be rather misplaced to deny the astonishing originality and insight of the themes contained in the *Economic and Philosophic Manuscripts*, but perhaps Marx's work in this respect is less important for its profundity and more important for its status as a representation of the myth of modernity. Just as Georg Simmel, Edmund Husserl and Milan Kundera similarly demonstrated the hold of one of the central myths of modernity (the problem of the products of reflexivity ossifying into reification), so much the same series of concerns, and much the same identified process, runs through the work of Marx. In the system of Marx, the central problem of modern times is exactly the contradiction between the ontological and anthropological fact that humanity is expressed through work, but the social and cultural fact that work is confronted by the worker in capitalism as something alien.

The implication is the collapse of humanity and the degradation of the worker to the level of base needs (in many ways it seems to be possible to read Marx's outrage on this point as a fear of ambivalence; the human should be distinct and bounded but capitalism for Marx means the blurring of the circumstances of humanity into the milieu of the animal). The reflexivity of labour leads to reification and the establishment of forms as something apart from social and cultural intervention. As such, the dehumanization of humanity is at once an ontological, an epistemological and a moral affair. But Marx took great care to avoid any kind of a monolithic representation of humanity. He knew that the establishment of reification over reflexivity and the barbarization of the subjects of capitalism was not the same for all classes. After all, 'It is true that labour produces wonderful things for the rich – but for the worker it produces privation. It produces palaces – but for the worker, hovels. It produces beauty – but for the worker, deformity' (Marx 1977: 65). Karl Marx continued to draw out yet more of the terrible consequences of the formal organization of labour: 'It replaces labour by machines, but it throws one section of the workers back to a barbarous type of labour, and it turns the other section into a machine. It produces intelligence – but for the worker, stupidity; cretinism' (Marx 1977: 65).

Marx is revealing and deconstructing the secrets of his world. He is seeking to know how the world works and he simply assumes that any understanding, just like the world itself, is self-sufficient. And his purpose is to overcome the increasing entrapment of the worker. The worker is trapped in the prison of forms because she or he is increasingly degraded to the status of an animal who treats the objective world as something immutable which simply must be (the world has become once again oppressive, restrictive nature; it ceases to be a creative and permissive society). The worker loses the ability to define the world for her or himself. 'As a result, therefore, man (the worker) only feels himself freely active in his animal functions – eating, drinking, procreating, or at most in his dwelling and in dressing-up etc.' (Marx 1977: 66). Marx pulled out the full implications of this situation in a typically brilliant dialectical aphorism. Marx said of the worker that 'in his human functions he no longer feels himself to be anything but an animal. What is animal becomes human and what is human becomes animal' (Marx 1977: 66). The worker is tied to a fixed identity which allows for no escape from the restraining and constraining effects of palaces and hovels, beauty and horror. The worker is tied to certainty without knowing. The identity of the working class is one of dehumanization and commodification.

The theme that modern social and cultural relationships are increasingly hemmed in by their own ossified and reified products remained important to Karl Marx throughout his work. The narrative is at the very heart of the discussion of commodity fetishism which is contained in the first volume of *Capital*. There, Marx makes the point that commodities are products of labour which, however, are apprehended by the worker as things with exchange values. The exchange values are relationships between independent objects rather than between the different amounts of labour power which were needed to make them. It is that objectivity which constitutes the basis of the commodity.

The commodity is something which is confronted as transcendental in relation to the labour which went into making it. Marx calls the commodity a 'mysterious thing 'and this for two reasons. Firstly because with the commodity 'the social character of men's labour appears to them as an objective character stamped upon the product of that labour' (Marx 1938: 42–3). Secondly, because 'the relation of the producers to the sum total of their own labour is presented to them as a social relation, existing not between themselves, but between the products of their labour' (Marx 1938: 43). In other words, the things of the world are apprehended and interpreted as independent. They are ossified, and therefore they are able to be defining of the meaning of labour rather than being defined by labour itself.

Consequently, Marx argued that with commodities, and in the relationships between commodities, the world ceases to be open to interpretation as a continuous product of human activity. Rather, the forms become self-sufficient objects. The

> existence of the things *qua* commodities, and the value relation between the products of labour which stamps them as commodities, is a definite social relation between men, that assumes, in their eyes, the fantastic form of a relation between things.
>
> (Marx 1938: 43)

This is the meaning of the fetishism of the commodity: social 'productions . . . appear as independent beings endowed with life, and entering into relation both with one another and the human race' (Marx 1938: 43).

As such, Marx's concept of commodity fetishism is in many ways trying to provide a way of coming to terms with a world which is essentially a contradiction; it is a social and a cultural production which is not understood as a social and a cultural production. That disjuncture is entirely explained by the tendency which is invested in products with exchange value to be commodified into forms which stand apart from conditions of production. The commodity is, then, a form which traps reflexivity, which reifies it through the imposition of a single meaning. Indeed, to participate in the milieu of the commodity is to establish yet further form over activity. Such participation is to demonstrate yet more the tragedy of modernity. And so therefore, it is to demonstrate yet further the overwhelming significance of the conflict in the heart of modernity.

So, Marx was distressed by the establishment of fixed identities over and above workers. Those identities were derived either from the brutalizing and cretinizing effects of the estranged capitalist arrangements, or from the formal status of the commodity as something seemingly without social and historical conditions of existence. Marx's story is one of the chaining of the universal species-being of humanity to a profoundly narrow and restricted time and place.

Man as a species sees 'himself as the actual, living species; because he treats himself as a *universal* and therefore a free being' (Marx 1977: 67).

Or rather, that is how the species should see itself. But thanks to estrangement the species is restricted and unfree. Indeed, the species is no longer able to freely express its intrinsic humanity. To this extent, the narrative contained in the work of Karl Marx might be used to reflect on the trajectory of modernity implied in the history of the novel outlined by Milan Kundera. It could be said that Kafka's Josef K. or the Land Surveyor in *The Castle* were anticipated in the story of the identification of the estranged and bounded worker of capitalism (I know that comment might seem silly to some people. However, and to repeat, I am dealing with myths of modernity and, in this light, Josef K. can be seen as an expression of themes contained in Marx).

But just as the Land Surveyor in *The Castle* does not give in to total despair because the prison is at least in part one of his own making, so a similar theme is expressed by Marx with Engels. The discussion in the *Communist Manifesto* of the revolutionizing impact of the bourgeoisie can be read as nothing other than an attempt to draw an optimistic and slightly comforting lesson from history. The lesson contains the moral that whilst contemporary fetishized relationships might seem to be frozen as if in ice, there is nevertheless hope that the table can be turned on the certainties of the bourgeoisie. To simply seek to know why and how the bourgeois milieu seems to be so solid is, in fact, to begin its demolition. Indeed, Marx and Engels thought that the initial demolition work would be carried out by the bourgeoisie itself; the bourgeoisie was to history what the wild children are to the fabricated dwelling of modernity.

Undoubtedly, the polemic rather gains an upper hand over theoretical and analytical rigour, but Marx and Engels were making a good point well when they said that 'Constant revolutionizing of production, uninter-rupted disturbance of all social conditions, everlasting uncertainty and agitation distinguish the bourgeois epoch from all earlier ones'. They famously continue: 'All fixed, fast-frozen relations, with their train of ancient and venerable prejudices and opinions are swept away, all new-formed ones become antiquated before they can ossify' (Marx and Engels 1967: 83). Of course, this passage contains a major contradiction.

Certainly, Marx and Engels declare that the bourgeoisie seeks to know the world and perpetually creates and recreates the human dwelling for itself (and thus it is something like an expression of the 'dwelling plight' identified by Martin Heidegger). But the difficulty is that Marx and Engels are actually perfectly sure that this is what the bourgeoisie is about. Paradoxically, they are certain that thanks to the bourgeoisie nothing is actually certain. Marx and Engels got around this problem by the relatively simple expedient of asserting that whilst the bourgeoisie might in fact be revolutionary, it is not revolutionary enough. In other words, they suggest that from the point of view of the Revolutionary Proletariat and, more specifically, from the point of view of the intellectuals, bourgeois relationships do indeed appear to be ossifications. Marx and Engels put class struggle and the dynamics of relationships of production in the place which Simmel later filled with life.

Marx and Engels know that the bourgeoisie had been able to profane the sacred and melt the solid; they know that this deconstruction of the once natural is the origin of the present boundaries. And to know that the modern arrangements are actually not natural and inevitable but that they might, indeed, be castles in the air, is to anticipate a time when they might be transcended. Because we got here by our own efforts, we can get ourselves out again. Short term pessimism goes hand in hand with longer term optimism. Perhaps that curious combination is also another of the defining traits of modernity.

For Marx it is possible to know everything and anything about the workers simply because they have been so completely trapped within the boundaries of form. Ironically then, the circumstances which produced the outrage and pessimism of Karl Marx were also the circumstances which allowed him to understand and optimistically interpret the actually existing social and cultural relationships. This is one of the greatest advantages of the construction and identification of fixed identities. Marx was operating as a reflexive intellectual who was seeking to know what the modern world meant, and consequently he saw the established certainties as nothing more than so many things to be transcended. But had he not been able to identify some established certainties, he would have been unable to say anything at all about the errors of actual conditions. Even less would he have been able to launch a moral attack in the name of some future.

For Marx, all the taken for granted certainties were things to be overcome through an intimation of things without bounds. But that intimation was quite inevitably decisively shaped by the identities which were to be overcome. It is only possible to transcend that which is. Consequently, the transcendental ideal is always and inevitably little more than an inversion of what is identified as existing (similarly, of course, freedom is simply that way of life which is better than this way of life; I have explored the meaning of freedom at greater length in Tester 1992).

Those things without the bounds of existing form were of two kinds. They involved the identification of a subject of reflexivity which was the opposite to the prevailing object of ossification (the Revolutionary

Proletariat in place of the workers and the working class) and a condition of reflexivity which was the opposite of the prevailing conditions of the fetish (Communism in place of commodified capitalist relationships). Both the Revolutionary Proletariat and Communism operated as categories which escaped empirical observation and knowledge. They were transcendental in relation to the actual. In many ways, they simply had to have that status of being beyond observation. After all, had it been possible to say 'there is the Proletariat' or 'there is Communism', the meanings of that which was supposedly without bounds would have been thoroughly bounded (a situation as logically absurd as the problem which emerged when Georg Simmel tried and failed to say what the category of life actually meant). Therefore, the Revolutionary Proletariat and Communism promised something like the final resolution of the modern conflict between reflexivity and reification, between knowing and certainty. They are fixed identities which can only be known through their achievement in the future. They cannot be the basis for knowledge and activity in the here and now because they are intrinsically and necessarily beyond the here and now.

Karl Marx's comments in the *Critique of the Gotha Programme* make it clear that Communism is a transcendence of the actual and an inversion of it. Moreover, it is noticeable that since Communism is taken to be the overcoming of form and ossification, its own characteristics are, in fact, more or less beyond the saying. Communism is an identity which will be vouchsafed by the future. From the point of view of the present, it is possible to be sure that the Communist identity will emerge, but it is rather less possible to unravel quite what that identity will actually involve. Put another way, Communist boundaries will emerge, but the nature of those boundaries are unknowable prior to the moment of their achievement. As such, they are without bounds. Communism is a transcendental identity. It is a condition without bounds which can only be known by us through reference to the bounds which it will render obsolete.

Marx makes it quite clear that Communist society cannot be known in isolation. Quite the contrary, Communist society can only be understood 'as it emerges from capitalist society; which is thus in every respect, economically, morally and intellectually, still stamped with the birth-marks of the old society from whose womb it emerges' (Marx 1942: 563). Communism is, then, a condition which is good simply and not least because it is called forth as a transcendence of the existing relationships which are interpreted as bad. Moreover, the way Marx founds Communism rather means that any ossifications which continue to trap and restrict the practices of self-definition can be blamed on the activities and lack of due care of the mother. The child itself is more or less quite blameless for any genetic or behavioural difficulties it might have. Marx made this absolution quite plain when he wrote that 'defects are inevitable in the first phase of communist society as it is when it has just emerged after prolonged birth pangs from capitalist society' (Marx 1942: 565).

Some of the difficulties which arise from the birth were intimated by Marx when he explored the nature and meaning of equal rights in bourgeois and Communist conditions. He shows that existing arrangements are illicit boundaries and that future arrangements are a going beyond of them. Marx criticizes notions of equal right as they are applied to the production and distribution of wealth. After all, to say that all individuals have equal rights is to fall into the trap of 'a bourgeois limitation'. He continues to spell out the nature of this limitation: 'It recognises no class differences, because everyone is only a worker like everyone else; but it tacitly recognises unequal individual endowment and thus productive capacity as natural privileges' (Marx 1942: 564).

The point and the problem is precisely that everyone is not equal. Some workers are more able than others, some workers need more than others: 'one worker is married, another not; one has more children than another and so on and so forth' (Marx 1942: 564). To bound all these individuals within a single standard (for example, the standard of equal rights) is, in fact, to define what it is to be human rather than to allow for self-definition. For Marx, it is to reify and to bound the meaning of existence. It is to say that all individuals should be 'taken from one *definite* side only, *e.g.*, in the present case are regarded *only as workers*, and nothing more seen in them, everything else being ignored' (Marx 1942: 564). The equality of the social subject means, for Marx, the inequality of the moral and economic subject. Consequently, the notion of right of the Communist society which emerges out of bourgeois society will have to be an inversion of the bourgeois bounds. As such, 'right instead of being equal would have to be unequal'.

But beyond that relatively straightforward, if not methodologically simple inversion, not much can be said about Communist society. Certainly, the Communist utopia can be identified as the milieu in which all divisions and all conflicts have been overcome. Certainly, it can be seen as the home of universality since all the boundaries of particularity have been transcended. But those postulates are, to say the least, rather grand in the sweep and vague in the detail. The point is, of course, that Marx found it quite impossible and inappropriate to make any comments about the details of the future condition which was to be without bounds. The reason is obvious. If Marx had said the details he would not only have fallen into the trap of bounding that which is properly without bounds but, and perhaps more significant politically, he would have been inserting the truths of Communist society into the circumstances of the bourgeois order. In other words, he would have been making Communism itself something to be overcome with the difficult birth of the new arrangements.

As such, the Communist future is left more or less unsaid. When Marx does try to say something definite about it, he rather fails. He can only define the identity of *that* condition to the extent that it is without the bounds of *this* condition. For example, in the *Critique of the Gotha Programme*, Marx reduces the complexities of social relationships to a series of assertions and a slogan. Marx writes that the 'higher phase of communist society' appears 'after the enslaving subordination of individuals under division of labour, and therewith also the antithesis between mental and physical labour, has vanished' (Marx 1942: 566). He continues to outline yet more of the boundaries which Communism will transcend. Communism appears 'after labour has become not merely a means to live but has become itself the primary necessity of life, after the productive capacities have also increased with the all-round development of the individual' (Marx 1942: 566). Only when all the existing bounds have been transcended, only when the actual forms of social relationships have been inverted and negated, 'only then can the narrow horizon of bourgeois right be fully left behind and society inscribe on its banners: from each according to his ability, to each according to his needs' (Marx 1942: 566).

But it was precisely that transcendental status of Communism which turned it into some kind of vision of freedom. It was freedom simply because it represented a movement without the bounds of bourgeois order. What the likes of Marx (and for that matter all the other reflexive intellectuals who turned their minds to such matters) did not realize was that it was exactly the possibility of the imagination of alternative arrangements which made the existing forms into ossifications and reifications in the first place. And neither did they fully acknowledge that without the assumption of existing reification, without the hermeneutic and historical certainties ostensibly embedded in the ossified forms, neither could there be any platform for the imagination of any alternatives. There would be nothing to be alternative to; there would be no prison from which to escape into freedom. Consequently, Communism might well be the inversion of capitalism and bourgeois order, but Communism is also the bastard child of capitalism. They actually reinforce, justify and formalize each other.

A fairly similar strategy of simple inversion into boundlessness can also be seen in the invocation of the Revolutionary Proletariat. Indeed, it might even be said that the proletariat is a quite unique category because it involves the self-transcendence of its own ossification. Whereas bourgeois order was transcended by something else (something called Communism), the existing proletariat is transcended by the proletariat turned revolutionary. In other words, part of the work of the bounded and estranged workers is to achieve their own transcendence. They were called by Marx to invert their reification and, instead, leap into the reflexivity of revolutionary consciousness. Put another way, the proletariat is a category which constructs the identity of the workers, and it is also a category by which the workers are potentially able to construct their identity for themselves. It is an identity of self-overcoming.

This dialectical nature of the category of the proletariat is demonstrated in the *Communist Manifesto*. In that text, the proletariat is a basis for bounded certainty in the here and now but also for the unbounded self-production of self-knowledge in the future.

On the one hand, the proletariat is bounded; it is an analytic category through which it is possible to understand and interpret the conditions of existence of the workers. To this extent, the proletariat represents the deadening effects of reification: 'Masses of labourers, crowded into the factory, are organized like soldiers. As privates of the industrial army they are placed under the command of a perfect hierarchy of officers and sergeants'. Marx and Engels continue to use metaphors of rigid regulation when talking of the proletariat as it is presently constituted by the workers: 'Not only are they slaves of the bourgeois class, and of the bourgeois State; they are daily and hourly enslaved by the machine, by the overlooker, and, above all, by the individual bourgeois manufacturer himself' (Marx and Engels 1967: 88).

But on the other hand, it is exactly this bounding of the workers which is the precondition of the revolutionary potential of the proletariat. Moreover, these boundaries provide the launching pad of the leap into the boundless. As such, the Revolutionary Proletariat represents a will to know the certainties of bourgeois order and, in so knowing, it deconstructs those certainties. The achievements of the Revolutionary Proletariat are absolutely impossible without the formal establishment of the achievements of the bourgeoisie. Indeed, when they start talking about the proletariat which has gone beyond the status of an analytic category bringing together all workers, and when they instead talk about the proletariat which has managed to reflect upon itself, Marx and Engels inevitably begin to reduce revolution to inversion. To this extent Marx and Engels say that 'In the conditions of the proletariat, those of old society at large are already virtually swamped' (Marx and Engels 1967: 92). In Simmel's terms, this passage might be read as a declaration of the eventual ability of life to overcome form; the passage at the very least identifies a cultural conflict between the old forms and the new activities.

The stuff of the transcendence carried out by the Revolutionary Proletariat is sketched a little more clearly by Marx and Engels when they make comments of the kind that: 'The proletarian is without property; his relation to his wife and children has no longer anything in common with the bourgeois family relations; modern industrial labour, modern subjection to capital ... has stripped him of every trace of national character' (Marx and Engels 1967: 92). Just as with the absent portrayal of Communism, then, the things which constitute the identity of the Revolutionary Proletariat are thoroughly determined by the actually existing arrangements. The Revolutionary Proletariat can only be known, and its identity can only be constructed, to the extent that it negates the arrangements which are currently taken largely for granted. The point is drawn out yet more when Marx and Engels continue their eulogy to the Revolutionary: 'Law, morality, religion, are to him so many bourgeois prejudices, behind which lurk in ambush just as many bourgeois interests' (Marx and Engels 1967: 92). To this extent then, the Revolutionary Proletariat is expressing the commitments of the culture of reflexive discourse. It is challenging all certainties and refusing to play the game of the equation of truth with social status or position. Instead, it is seeking to know the basis of certainty and deconstructing, revealing for all to see the artificiality of any and all statements which are approached as if they are natural.

However, once again, and just as with Communism, quite what the Revolutionary Proletariat looks like, quite what it does and quite what its goal means, is left extremely vague. It might well be true that 'The proletarians have nothing to lose but their chains. They have a world to win' (Marx and Engels 1967: 120–2). But the nature of that world and the identity of the people who will live in it are left to be known. About the identities it is impossible, and perhaps more importantly quite illicit, to be certain.

These rather imprecise implications of the identity of the proletariat have been drawn out in an interesting way by Jean François Lyotard. He argues that the proletariat has the status of a Kantian Idea in Reason. Basically, when Kant proposed the significance of Ideas in Reason, he was trying to make the point that it is possible to rationally postulate certain identities or things even though they are quite beyond sensual perception. For example, Kant said that the notion of eternity is an Idea in Reason. He once wrote that when we talk about eternity 'We are dealing (or playing) here simply with Ideas which reason itself creates, the objects of which (if it possesses any) lie completely beyond our field of vision' (Kant 1963: 75–6). So, Kant is trying to make the point that it is possible to talk about eternity and to say that eternity means certain things even though eternity is, virtually by definition, quite beyond the human 'field of vision'. Eternity can be represented (but not presented) because it is an Idea which is derived from the operation of reason. It is possible to postulate eternity because reason suggests the category of eternity and not necessarily because eternity actually exists. Indeed, the existence or otherwise of eternity is quite unknowable by us.

Now, according to Lyotard, Marx's proletariat also has the status of an Idea in Reason. It too is derived solely from the operations of the forms of knowledge and understanding. As such Lyotard makes the perfectly valid point that 'Nobody has ever seen a proletariat (Marx said this): you can observe working-classes, certainly, but they are only part of the observable society'. But, Lyotard continues, 'It's impossible to argue that this part of society is the incarnation of a proletariat, because an Idea in general has no presentation, and *that is the question of the sublime*' (Lyotard 1989: 23). With the reference to the sublime, and with the hint that the proletariat represents the sublime because it cannot be presented, Lyotard is perhaps going rather too far. Certainly, it can be said that the proletariat (just like Communism) implies a transcendence of the existing boundaries. This much is by now a common-place. But that does not at all mean that the transcendence necessarily involves a leap into the sublime as such. Quite the contrary, it simply involves a leap into a milieu which is imagined as without bounds (and which is therefore imagined as sublime by those who remain within bounds) simply because the boundaries which constitute the point of imagination (and of the agent of the imagination) are inverted and negated. The proletariat is not necessarily sublime and neither is Communism; it is simply the identity of an alternative world which is seen as transcendent in relation to this world.

One implication of the foregoing discussion might be that Karl Marx's work contains a kind of hesitant, unrealized, embryonic anticipation of post-modernity. It might be possible to interpret the identities of the proletariat and Communism as intimations of a condition without bounds. In itself that might well be true. But Marx was not moving beyond the bounds of the modernity which was constructed in the wake of deconstruction of natural artifice. In many ways, he was desperately trying to reinforce the foundations of the modern house which he had left open to the destructive impact of the elements. Arguably, what can be found in the work of Marx is not an attempt to transcend the modern but instead, an attempt to turn away from the existential abyss which seemingly lurks outside of it. Put another way, Karl Marx is an emphatically modern thinker.

Basically, Marx knew that social institutions and arrangements do not exist by nature but that, instead, they only seem to exist by nature because they are ossified and reified human productions. His work quite clearly contains the awareness that the world only makes sense to the extent that it is forgotten that the categories of meaning are themselves contingent. In this way, Marx potentially came face to face with a meaningless world (he almost approached the edge, to recall Michel Foucault's lovely phrase, of the glittering abyss of meaning). But he did not fall over the edge. Indeed, he might not have even looked into the abyss. Instead of pushing the possibility of transcendence and the possibility of unsayability to its very limit (that is, instead of jumping into the sublime milieu which lacks all places and all direction), Marx instead harnessed the story of the transcendence of form to a story about history.

Marx wanted to know the basis of the existing forms, but he was only confident enough to do that, and he only had the existential commitment to do that, because he never questioned the certainties ostensibly contained within history. Ultimately, the thought of Marx might well contain necessary and fascinating silences, but he was only prepared to sanction the blanks because he was certain that with the passage of history they would be filled with meaning. Whatever else Marx could not, or did not, say, he was nevertheless convinced that: 'What the bourgeoisie . . . produces, above all, is its own grave-diggers. Its fall and the victory of the proletariat are equally inevitable' (Marx and Engels 1967: 94).

The intrinsic modernity of Marx's thought was further reinforced by his use of the notion of the proletariat. For Marx, the proletariat was something to be achieved at least in part through political activity in the present moment. As such, Marx implicitly reduced some of the identity of the proletariat to forms of bounded action and meaning. For example, in the chapter of the *Communist Manifesto* on 'Proletarians and Communists', Marx and Engels not only reduce the interest and identity of the Revolutionary Proletariat to the activities of the organized Party, but they also reduce the aims of the Party to ten policy objectives (Marx and Engels 1967: 104–5) Consequently, the destiny of the proletariat itself became a form. It might have been a form with a fundamentally mysterious core, but it was a form nevertheless. The implication should be obvious; whereas Marx, Engels and all the Communists rested the hopes for reflexivity and the overcoming of reification in the proletariat (such that it can be known that 'In bourgeois society, therefore, the past dominates the present; in Communist society, the present dominates the past' [Marx and Engels 1967: 97–8]), later intellectuals saw the proletariat itself as a form which had to be transcended.

The overcoming of the form and identity of the proletariat has been expressed by André Gorz amongst many others. What is interesting in Gorz's work is how his enthusiasm to rescue reflexivity and self-definition from reification and definition from outside virtually means that he is unable to say very much at all. He says much less than Karl Marx did not say. Certainly, Gorz rejects the usefulness of identities such as that of the proletariat, but when he then attempts to provide some categories for an understanding of the order of things, the vacuity is quite astonishing. Gorz refuses to use the concept of the proletariat either as a description of an existing social group or, indeed, as an invocation of the subject of revolutionary action.

According to André Gorz, Marx's calling forth and imagination of (what Gorz prefers to call) socialism, rested on two assumptions. Firstly, Gorz says that Marx thought that socialism 'was carried by a class of proletarianized social producers that formed a virtual majority of the population'. Secondly, Gorz says that Marx assumed that the proletariat 'was defined, in essence, by conscious rejection of its class being' (Gorz 1982: 66). Gorz continues quite rightly to point out Marx's dialectical appreciation of the proletariat. As Gorz writes, 'The proletariat was the only class, and the first in history, which had no interest but to cancel its class being by destroying the external constraints by which it had been constituted' (Gorz 1982: 66).

Now, according to Gorz, the ossifications which have confronted the proletariat have become so overwhelming that the project of self-transcendence has collapsed. Firstly, and in contradiction to Marx's confidence in history, Gorz argues that 'A class whose social activity yields no power does not have the means to take power, nor does it feel called upon to do so' (Gorz 1982: 67). The proletariat is unable and unprepared to overcome form because it does not see reification as a prison. It simply sees reification as the way things must be. Secondly, Gorz suggests that to define individuals by reference to their work is misplaced. Thanks to new technologies and new procedures, 'It is no longer possible for workers to identify with "their" work or "their" function . . . Everything now appears to take place outside themselves. "Work" itself has become a quantum of reified activity awaiting and subjugating the "worker" ' (Gorz 1982: 67). As such, to follow Marx and to refer identity to work is, in fact, to reinforce the dominance of ossification. It is to reconfirm the supremacy of the dead past over the living present.

Consequently, André Gorz tries to operate beyond the boundaries of the identities of labour and class. He suggests that such a movement has a number of advantages. It not only allows for the development of a better analysis of social and economic relations, but it also helps analysis avoid taken for granted assumptions. For Gorz, the abandonment of the identity of the proletariat is a very good thing indeed. After all, 'For over a century the idea of the proletariat has succeeded in masking its own unreality. This idea is now as obsolete as the proletariat itself' (Gorz 1982: 67). Gorz continues to suggest why the idea is as obsolete as the reality to which it allegedly refers: 'in place of the productive collective worker of old, a non-class of non-workers is coming into being' (Gorz 1982: 67). Clearly, Gorz is looking beyond boundaries and thus looking straight into the abyss of meaning. His world after the proletariat is not a world which is possessed of its own positive meanings, it is simply a world in which the existing forms and meanings have been negated. But with Gorz it is a negation without purpose whereas for Marx it was always and fundamentally a negation with purpose.

André Gorz seems to have forgotten the point that the milieu without bounds need only be intimated. It does not need to be embraced since to do so is like embracing a grain of sand. As such, the central identity of Gorz's 'post-industrial' society is, actually, a non-identity. Gorz has gone beyond the boundaries of meaning and ended up nowhere. All he can see is a negation, a 'non-class of post-industrial proletarians'. Gorz suggests that this non-class knows itself but it cannot be certain of itself. Or at least, it cannot be certain except negatively: 'The only certainty, as far as they are concerned, is that they do not feel they belong to the working class, or to any other class . . . neo-proletarians are basically non-workers temporarily doing something that means nothing to them' (Gorz 1982: 70–1). It is rather tempting to wonder how André Gorz could possibly know this, even more how he could be certain enough to write a book about it.

Basically, Gorz's work on the identity of the proletariat represents a caricature of the conflict in modern culture. Marx developed the boundless category of the proletariat to provide some basis and constituency for the transcendence of the forms of bourgeois order; Gorz has encountered Marx's work as a historical artifact which has itself become ossified (the legacy of the technical enterprise called Marxism and, especially, Marxism-Leninism). Therefore, Gorz has looked at the categories of Marx's thought through the hermeneutic commitments of reflexive discourse and interpreted them as a catalogue of reifications to be deconstructed. That deconstruction more or less schematically involved an inversion of Marx's categories and a revelation of their artificiality (Gorz was trying to claim a kind of hermeneutic freedom from Marx's system). As such, whereas Marx talks about the objective and subjective class of the proletariat which is defined through its relationship to the means of production and through its political organization, Gorz sees instead a non-class of the proletariat for which work means nothing and politics means a reflection on impotence (Gorz 1982: 72).

A similar kind of hermeneutic move, although to different ends and for different purposes, can be seen in the work of Jean Baudrillard. Especially in his rather interesting book, *In the Shadow of the Silent Majorities* (Baudrillard 1983), it is possible to find an interpretation of the post-modern which is little more than a transcendence of the expressions and identities of the modern. Quite typically then, and just like André Gorz, Baudrillard has tried to move without bounds. But perhaps Baudrillard does it better than Gorz. In particular, Baudrillard has some very pertinent things to say about the nature and the meaning of the often invoked class of the masses.

The point is, of course, that in the dominant narratives of the modern, the masses were frequently understood as one of the essential agents of societal activity and transformation. Baudrillard talks about the identity of the modern masses in his own inimitable style (perhaps Baudrillard is one of the most notable amongst those who take a change of style and ornamentation for a change of the structures as such). Quite accurately, and in a way which implicitly emphasizes and illustrates the hermeneutic possibilities of boundaries, Baudrillard writes that 'According to their imaginary representation, the masses drift somewhere between passivity and wild spontaneity, but always as a potential energy, a reservoir of the social and of social energy' (Baudrillard 1983: 2). For example, and to illustrate Baudrillard's point, the working class is understood as either totally estranged and wholly under the sway of bourgeois ideological and physical force, or the working class is transformed into a Revolutionary Proletariat which is identified by nothing so much as its wild action which constitutes an energy which will throw off the products of commodity fetishism and dead labour.

On the one hand, the modern narratives interpret the identity of the masses as something imposed from outside, but on the other hand, the identity is interpreted as coming from inside. Baudrillard realizes this double identity when he says that the masses are 'today a mute referent, tomorrow, when they speak up and cease to be the "silent majority", a protagonist of history' (Baudrillard 1983: 2). However, when Baudrillard develops these useful and very stimulating points, and when he turns to an interpretation of the stakes and the nature of post-modernity, he operates in terms of the conventions of absence.

Whereas the modern interpretations and identities emphasize the potential of the wild spontaneity, or at least the profound social energy of the masses, Baudrillard goes beyond those boundaries and creates an identity of the masses as little more than couch potatoes. The modern masses were about actual or potential, realized or latent energy. The post-modern masses could not be more different. Baudrillard does not deny that the post-modern masses have strength, but he does deny that the strength is a strength of doing. Quite the contrary, according to Baudrillard the identity of the post-modern masses is derived from their inertia. According to Baudrillard the strength of these masses 'is a specific inertial strength, whose effectivity differs from that of all those schemas of production, radiation and expansion according to which our imaginary functions, even in its wish to destroy those same schemas' (Baudrillard 1983: 3). They also serve the revolution who sit and watch football on the television.

Baudrillard's point is that the modern masses were tied to identities of production and of becoming (i.e. they were understood as going from *this* to *that*). But the post-modern masses possess none of this active strength and identity. They are simply inertia. Consequently, they are not the producer or the site of meaning, rather they are the consumer and the negation of meaning. As such, Baudrillard proposes that in terms of the class of the masses at least the days of the usefulness of the modern boundaries have gone. 'There is no longer any polarity . . . in the mass. This is what causes that vacuum and inwardly collapsing effect in all those systems which survive on the separation and distinction of poles (two, or many more in complex systems)' (Baudrillard 1983: 6).

The discourses on the proletariat and Communism and the masses can be taken as prime illustrations of the kind of conflict in modern culture, the kind of culture in modernity, which Georg Simmel and the others were trying to grasp. On the one hand, modern interpretations and practices had to be able to point to some fixed identities in the world. Had those formal characteristics of things been undiscovered, or perhaps it is better to say, left uninvented (had content been left without form), then the world would not have made sense. After all, the primary principle of the modern deconstruction of natural artifice is the declaration that meaning is a social and a cultural product; it is made and not given. These identities had to be fixed and taken for granted or else social locations and directions would have been incomprehensible. But, and on the other hand, those fixed identities were themselves very susceptible to reflexive deconstruction.

Ironically, the identities which created meaning, which had to be taken for granted, actually could not be left to be taken for granted. Had they been put beyond deconstruction, they would have represented so many obstacles in the way of the resolute and remorseless modern demolition of everything which is assumed to exist by nature. This contradiction is the nub of the conflict between reflexivity and reification. The two thrusts of the modern enterprises are actually quite irreconcilable. One expression of the recognition of the intrinsic irreconcilability of the conflict is the identification of a condition of post-modernity.

Chapter 3

Nostalgia

The will to certainty implies the creation and imposition of fixed identities. As such, it implies also the enhancement of the place and importance of the human in the world. Since we know for sure what we are, who we are, and where we are, so we know also that the world holds no ultimate mysteries for us. Our fixation and the promises of the future mean that we will not be tripped by any potholes in the road to freedom. But the problem is that those very certainties are apprehended by some, by those who are committed to the claims and requirements of the culture of reflexive discourse, as so many prisons. Consequently, everything fixed is something to be transcended. Ironically, the certainty of our place and destiny is also the basis of a profound confidence to challenge the things which, for some, can only be understood as illicitly taken for granted.

Meanwhile, the will to know implies the transcendence of any fixed and evidently formal identities. It implies not certainty, but relentless movement; it implies not the safe havens of ascription but, instead, the never ending and never consummated struggle for achievement. The will to know implies ceaseless self-definition rather than the acceptance of any definition from outside (and a fixed identity is precisely such an externally imposed meaning). But the end result and the purpose of the achievement of self-definition, of reflexivity over and above the things which are consequently identified as reifications, cannot be said. After all, to identify some end goal and to know its meaning in advance is actually to ascribe certainty and to define the meaning of things (this is in part one of the many problems contained in Kant's essay on Enlightenment; it is also one of the reasons why the essay is so rich. Kant's text contains the very major problem that Enlightenment might logically mean the transcendence of Enlightenment itself; see Kant 1970). It is to deny the full implications of the will to know.

Consequently, whereas the will to certainty makes the human large or at least central in relation to all the other things of the world (because the human is the axial centre which holds all else in orbit around it; the will to certainty holds to the view that the things of the universe revolve around the stationary, always the same, and beyond question, centre signified by Man), the will to know makes the human small and perpetually peripheral (it means that, to recall Yeats' poem *The Second Coming*, 'the falcon cannot hear the falconer').

The two hermeneutic responses to the fact of living in a fabricated rather than a natural world, responses which are equally legitimate and equally pure (the one is not a corrupted nor a diseased version of the other) are actually more or less intrinsically in contradiction to each other. In many ways, the appearance of the contradiction and the conflict can be taken as a sure sign of the emergence of modernity. But it should also be stressed that the conflict is actually quite irresolvable from within the intellectual, formal and practical conditions of modernity. In order to reconcile the divergent aims and claims of the will to certainty and the will to know, it is necessary to intimate a transcendence of the arrangements and relationships of modernity.

That is in many ways exactly the nature of the debates on post-modernity. They are faltering or exuberant attempts to overcome the contradiction between certainty and knowing. Post-modernity does not however mean the once and for all reconciliation of the contradiction. It simply intimates the dialectical transcendence of it.

The reflection of this thoroughly irresolvable modern dilemma runs through many of the most important modern myths. For example, it is arguably something by way of the motivating insight of the existentialism which turned around the problems of the certainty of knowing and the knowing of certainty. The insight and appeal of the best existentialist literature (invariably the novels rather than the more consciously academic-philosophical work; this is especially true of Sartre whose novels reveal a clarity and a brevity which is woefully lacking from his more self-consciously Important Treatises) resides in the intuited but possibly never clearly grasped fact that the certainty of knowing and the knowing of certainty are actually quite incompatible. (As an example of this point, it is worth comparing the attitudes and practices of the characters of the Autodidact and Anton Roquentin in *Nausea*; Sartre 1965.) Hence also, perhaps, the existentialist attempt to outmanoeuvre the difficulty by pushing the drama of existence inside into the heads of the protagonists and outside into wilful but frequently utterly vacuous acts. In any case, existentialism can be read as a myth of modernity which attempts to say something for sure about the position of the human in the modern order of things.

But more obviously, more originally and perhaps even more profoundly, the reflection on the difficult position of the human in the artificial modern world is contained in the legend of Faust (for brilliant discussions of Goethe's version of the Faust legend and its importance in modernity, see Berman 1983 and Redner 1982. Redner quite rightly also pays attention to the Fausts of Marlowe and Mann). Even a quick survey of some of the themes in the story of Faust can reveal some of the paradoxes, problems and possibilities of modernity.

Faust is modern enough to know that certainty is barren. Of course, that sense of the exhaustion of everything which has been accepted since time immemorial is very significantly exacerbated by the fact that Faust is an extremely self-conscious and jealous reflexive intellectual. Faust knows that certainty is boring and nothing other than a restriction of what self-sufficient humanity might achieve if it is released from its prisons and given free rein (although the eventual irony of the Faust story is that the prison of form can only be escaped if humanity gives up self-sufficiency). In the Faust story, the initially artificial world created by the will to know has already become rather like a taken for granted home of certainty. It has consequently been transformed from a place of wild debauches (or at least of the possibility of anything going) into a jail house of the soul. Faust is trapped by the forms which previously allowed him to express life. For example, Christopher Marlowe has his Doctor Faustus ponder with weary apathy: 'Is to dispute well logic's chiefest end? / Affords this art no greater miracle? / Then read no more, thou hast attain'd that end' (Marlowe 1976: 276).

Marlowe's Faustus asks the question but he cannot stop reading and thinking. After all, with Faustus it is possible to see an expression and a reflection of the spirit and ethic of the modern intellectual. Marlowe's character can never stop wanting to know. He might be bored and dejected, but still Faustus is driven by the will to deconstruct the products of previous exploits. The products have now come to take on the matter of fact certainty of nature. And anything which is confronted as nature demands to be known (Marlowe's Faustus is in many ways a partner of Bacon). In particular, and in a confrontation with a reification of humanity which even now has not been entirely dealt with, Marlowe's Doctor Faustus wants to know how women and men can be released from the prison of their decaying physical form. He confronts the ultimate reification of death. Even in the face of doubt and boredom, Faustus is confident enough to try to tackle the old metaphysical chestnut of immortality. In comparison with that struggle to know of death, Faustus considers all certainty to be trivial. Here, Faustus is talking to himself; he is reflexively interrogating and applauding his own conceits and ambitions: 'A greater subject fitteth Faustus' wit: / . . . Be a physician Faustus, heap up gold, / And be eterniz'd for some wondrous cure' (Marlowe 1976: 276).

By the time Marlowe's Doctor Faustus has become Goethe's Faust, the struggle to practise reflexivity and thus to escape any reification has become more and more pronounced. Goethe's Faust is also bored with the formal architecture of certainty (so that, perhaps, the soaring Gothic architecture of the study represents the restricted and narrowed hopes of humanity). Faust has achieved a thoroughly ironic certainty and confidence. He knows that any absolute certainty is at best chimerical and at worst fraudulent (here, Goethe is anticipating part of Weber's story of science, the part which says that the purpose of science being the achievement of its own obsolescence): 'And well I know that ignorance is our fate, / and this I hate' (Goethe 1949: 43).

By way of adding a further illustration to the story of literature told by Milan Kundera it is worth comparing the Faustus of Marlowe with the Faust of Goethe. Christopher Marlowe has Faustus transcend boredom and entrapment through a mixture of fireworks, sex and adventure. But later Goethe tells a tale of the deliberate intellectually inspired struggle to transcend all the reifications of form. Faustus goes out, whereas Faust more significantly initially goes in, deep inside himself.

Perhaps this difference can help explain the importance in Goethe's version of the story of the scene when Faust translates the Bible so that it rings true for his own conditions of existence. Goethe's Faust does not find the translation a terribly easy task. But in the end he plumps for a version of Creation which is little more than a self-image of the self-definitions of the modern imagination: 'I write, "In the beginning was the Deed" ' (Goethe 1949: 71. It is this passage which provides the central problem of Harry Redner's splendid book.). Faust's translation is quite clearly open to interpretation as part of a massive attempt to restate the case for reflexivity. For Faust, being is about doing and making. It is about active and determined production rather than passive and quiet consumption (whereas Marlowe's Faustus was prepared to consume the images and the objects which were given to him, Goethe's Faust wants to play a part in their production). But the price of that struggle is a refusal to accept the legitimacy of anything and everything which is taken for granted.

The difficulty which confronted Goethe's Faust was that he lost all

place and fixed direction in the world with the deconstruction of his own
certainty. The Deed might well be the beginning, but if it is then it has no
definite location or purpose. The difficulty was exacerbated yet more by
Faust's rather desperate attempt to create new possibilities for reflexivity
from out of the traditions of the past achievements. Faust sees the past as
a resource for the present and the future.

In this respect, a significant moment in the story is the scene where
Faust goes out walking but feels trapped by the applause of the crowd.
The crowd is thanking the good Doctor for the efforts he made long ago
with his father to alleviate the town from the worst of a plague (Goethe
1949: 64–7). Faust's problem is that the clapping hands are like so many
death knells. He responds to them by beating a hasty retreat from the
memories of what used to be. He deliberately struggles to move without
the bounds of all previous certainty. But then he ceases to know exactly
who and where he is. Faust's relentless will to know has produced only
doubt upon doubt. In the face of his glorious past, Faust confronts an
existential crisis. He asks and quite fails to answer the question: 'Shall I
then rank with gods? Too well I feel / My kinship with the worm, who
bores the soil' (Goethe 1949: 52).

The only viable response to the defining gratitude of the crowd is for
Faust to try to forget the question of whether he is like a god or like a
worm. The attempt to forget involves a mixture of the restatement of
self-sufficient doing (so that there is not time to ask the question of the
status of existence) and a deft but ultimately disastrous passing of the
buck of the responsibility for certainty to someone else. (In these terms,
Faust's turn to Mephistopheles is a fine example of the cowardice which
Immanuel Kant had already bewailed as one of the greatest obstacles in
the way of universal Enlightenment; Kant 1970.)

Basically, Goethe's Faust is representing nothing other than the
hermeneutic and moral problems which are thrown up by modernity. The
will to know which is the representation of the interests of the intellectuals
implies nothing other than the possibility of the discovery of a complete
and terrible abyss of meaning without the walls of the constructions of
modernity. Faust had come face to face with the possibility that
everything which was accepted as self-evident might be quite meaningless if not utterly futile. His horror at the applause of the crowd reflects a
wider fear of what lurks outside of the consolations and distractions of
tradition and the cheap glory which cultural relationships has on offer.
Faust is appalled at the prospect that outside of the rituals of tradition
there might be no source of guarantees. But his horror also reflects the
attitude of the intellectual that tradition too is terrible.

The Faust story as told by Goethe demonstrates the difficulty of modernity that to know everything means also to know that everything is at least in principle of a purely temporary legitimacy. That which has not been deconstructed today remains to be deconstructed tomorrow. And the will to know succeeds precisely to the extent that the pool of the things which remain is gradually and yet methodically emptied. Goethe is, arguably, revealing some of the stakes of the situation which appear when the order of things is made and fabricated as opposed to found. Goethe is also showing that for some people the modern making is simply forgotten (they are happy to applaud memories because the memories still hold good; they do not realize that the memories will always hold good all the time they applaud) whilst for others, for the reflexive intellectuals, the story of the making simply must be dredged up at all costs. For the intellectuals, certainty is just too boring to countenance.

Faust for one knows that certainty is boring. For him it is a prison which restricts and defines. But he knows also that without that certainty nothing would be open to the saying, the knowing or even quite possibly, the doing. Without reified forms there could actually be no reflexivity. But without reflexivity the dwelling of the human could not be fabricated. Faust knows that without the struggle of social and cultural activity against itself, humanity will be for the foreseeable future confined within the bounded forms of reification. He knows that reification can be and therefore (after Kant) should be transcended, but the results of that overcoming might not be an entirely good thing. Ultimately, the turn to Mephistopheles represents a failure of nerve on Faust's part; he wants to move without bounds but he wants someone or something to hold his hand. As such, he was not moving without bounds at all.

On the one hand, Goethe's Faust knows that he is in principle sufficient unto himself; he knows that he is defining of his own identity. Faust knows that, as a later poet said, without himself, 'Things fall apart; the centre cannot hold' (Yeats 1982). But, on the other hand, his identity as the kind of individual he has become is intuited as a restriction; it is dull and uninteresting. The fixed identity is something to be overcome. Faust is impaled on the dilemma of whether he is in fact a god or a worm. And in the end Goethe can actually provide no answer either way. Faust is certain that without him the world would fall apart, but he might not be entirely sure that his identity today will be also his identity tomorrow.

By way of assisting with the contextualization of these points, it can be said that 'existence is modern in as far as it is saturated by the "without us, a deluge" feeling' (Bauman 1991: 7). Indeed, Faust confronts this possibility of the deluge but only to turn his back on it, only to find an excuse not to peer into the abyss of the deluge. The excuse is called Mephistopheles with his promise that ultimate meaning will be found in the future after deconstruction has been achieved (although Mephistopheles did not let on that when deconstruction is achieved Faust must die and thus overcome his own identity once and for all). By emphasizing the dilemmas of Faust, Goethe seems to want the modern institutions and arrangements to know of the possibility of the deluge. He might even have written a parable which tells us that the deluge must be confronted. But he does offer some kind of despairing hope that we might never be swept up to fall into the abyss of meaning.

Instead of having to come face to face with the abyss, we can carry out massive projects which will distract us, or we can locate the moment of deluge in some point of a tomorrow which will never come. Or we can become utopian and identify some moment in the future when the deluge will simply not be something to be feared; when it will, instead, be nothing other than a giant cleansing shower. In all of these ways, the order of things can be known to be modern, but it can also be taken for granted as the more or less sturdy place which will protect the inhabitants of the modern from the storms which rage on the outside of meaningfulness.

This kind of move can be found in the work of Karl Marx. On the one hand he deconstructed all certainty to reveal the full horror of the abyss of meaning, but he then pulled the frozen onlookers away from the precipice by telling them that everything would be all right in the end. In this way, the order of things could be both known as an artifice and yet assumed to be adequate for what was about to happen. Marx forces a confrontation with the despair which lurks outside the front door of modernity. But then he puts a paternal arm around his audience to tell them not to worry. The future, and a commitment to the practices required by the future, will vouchsafe the possibility of meaning. As an example of all of this, it is useful to read the short speech which Marx delivered in April 1856 at a dinner commemorating the anniversary of the *People's Paper* (Marx 1973. The speech is also discussed by Marshall Berman; see Berman 1983: 19–21).

At the very beginning of the speech, Karl Marx told his listeners that recent events in Europe had revealed the possibility of the social and cultural cataclysm. He said that whilst the 'so-called revolutions of 1848 were but poor incidents – small fractures and fissures in the dry crust of European society', they had nevertheless demonstrated something of quite massive magnitude. Quite simply, the events 'denounced the abyss. Beneath the apparently solid surface they betrayed oceans of liquid matter, only needing expansion to rend into fragments continents of hard rock' (Marx 1973: 299). Now, admittedly, there is more than a hint here that Marx had read a rather florid geology book, but he does convey the sense of apocalypse very well. Essentially, Karl Marx is saying that it is possible to know of the truths which are hidden beneath the surface forms; it is possible to know that the prevailing certainties and reifications are about to be exploded into so many pieces.

But it is instructive to see what happens next. Just as Faust's confidence gave out in the face of the abyss, so does Karl Marx's. The possibility of complete reflexivity and flux in the present is too much for him to bear and countenance. Complete reflexivity might well be, indeed it is, permissible for the future, but for the present complete reflexivity (all content, no form; all movement, no fixed identities) is simply too much. And of course, the beauty of the future for this particular problem is that it is always some point on the distant and ever-receding horizon. By definition the future is always to be attained. The predicate for the modern faith in the future is precisely the inherent impossibility of the attainability of the future. Hence, the unattainability of the objects and the conditions of modern faith.

Marx conjures the abyss only to draw certainties out of its destiny. All the intimations of the abyss actually reveal is a certain future: 'Noisily and confusedly they proclaimed the emancipation of the proletarian, i.e. the secret of the nineteenth century, and of the revolution of that century' (Marx 1973: 299). By the end of the speech, Marx was allowing himself to say even more. Once again he is demonstrating the fundamental and inescapable modernity of his thought. Marx is a primary protagonist of the will to know, but he does not therefore intimate a post-modern condition without the bounds of the modern. Rather, he goes to the very edge of the precipice and quickly pulls back to find the comfort of certainty (that is, a long term will to certainty) in history. Marx tells his audience that in the Middle Ages in Germany, a secret group used to paint a red cross on the doors of houses inhabited by people who were to be revenged by the populace for their part in 'the misdeeds of the ruling class'. The red cross acted as a sign of fixed identity. Marx continued to tell the audience: 'All the houses of Europe are now marked with the mysterious red cross. History is the judge – its executioner, the proletarian' (Marx 1973: 300).

As such, it is possible to propose that the work of Karl Marx can be read as an especially clear expression of modernity as futurity. Marx works around the abyss of meaning and the felt need to deconstruct fixed identities by locating all certainty in some future condition. The future is nearly everything. His work contains barely a hint of any respect for the past. With remarkable integrity, Marx refuses to avoid the more problematic consequences of the will to know. He does not hide behind the safe and secure certainties which were ostensibly bequeathed to him by tradition. He knows that tradition is a form which is an affront to reflexivity and which is, moreover, quite incompatible with a relentless deconstruction of the taken for granted (after all, the very point of tradition is that it is simply there, seemingly always and forever). Marx responds to the order of things of modernity by designing the blueprint for an even better order in the future. And that means that the past has to be destroyed and left behind once and for all.

For Marx, the past and the traditional is simply a milieu of superstition and immaturity (to recall Kant's imperative of Enlightenment) which must be demolished in the name of the modern institutions and arrangements. Consequently, the groups which practise and believe the taken for granted become problems from the point of view of the commitment to the future. In the words of Marshall Berman they are 'people who are in the way – in the way of history, of progress, of development; people who are classified, and disposed of, as obsolete' (Berman 1983: 67. Berman makes this point as part of a discussion on Faust as a modernizer aiming towards the future).

These kinds of themes are very clear in Marx's essays on India. Marx rejoices in the fact that the globalization of capitalism through the British Empire has finally crushed the traditional practices, meanings and social relationships which were in the way of the march to the future (and it was precisely the confidence in the future which made Marx certain that indigenous forms were obstacles to be overcome). For a moment in one of the essays on India it looks as if Marx the great protagonist of modernity is unhappy that so many old ways have been destroyed. For a little while it looks as if he is allowing himself to shed a tear for the uprooted milieu of tradition. He says that the extension of British rule in India has consequences which are 'sickening . . . to human feeling' (Marx 1973a: 306). For Marx, the pulling of India into the milieu of modernity is terrible in this emotive kind of way precisely because it involves the destruction of indigenous relationships. British rule is throwing India over the edge of the abyss of meaning. According to Karl Marx British rule (and therefore British capitalism) in India has resulted in 'myriads of industrious patriarchal and inoffensive social organizations disorganized and dissolved into their units, thrown into a sea of woes, and their individual members losing at the same time their ancient form of civilization and their hereditary means of subsistence' (Marx 1973a: 306).

Here, Marx is confronting the hermeneutic and existential consequences of the deconstruction of natural artifice. He is showing that the manifestation and the practice of a will to know means the destruction of any and all certainties. But Marx does not therefore throw up his arms in horror and turn away in the face of the utter meaninglessness of everything which is done. Quite the contrary. He is committed to the futurity of the fabrication of an improved order of things and, therefore, he believes that it might actually be a splendid thing if the traditions of India are forced over the edge. Karl Marx's tears for the time honoured traditions, for the taken for granted, very quickly turn out to be the tears of a crocodile.

After all, and for Marx this is virtually justification enough for enforced modernity, there is another side to the almost idyllic picture of pleasant relationships and productions. The problem of India, the problem which modernity could and should solve, was precisely that indigenous conditions defined humanity rather than allowed humanity to be defining of itself. In other words, Marx finally glories in the deconstruction of the natural artifice in India precisely because, from his point of view, such reified forms are an illicit imprisonment of self-sufficiency. As Marx says, 'we must not forget that these idyllic village communities, inoffensive though they may appear, had always been the solid foundation of Oriental despotism' (Marx 1973a: 306). Marx continues to decry the indigenous forms on grounds which recall immediately the basis of Kant's plea for Enlightenment. Marx urges his modern European audience never to forget that the forms of India 'restrained the human mind within the smallest possible compass, making it the unresisting tool of superstition, enslaving it beneath traditional rules, depriving it of all grandeur and historical energies' (Marx 1973a: 306).

Basically, then, Marx bids farewell and good riddance to anything and everything which has become established as a reified form. Indeed, the meaningfulness of Marx's enterprise is located in the very extent to which the relentless transcendence of form implies an alternative future. It was precisely the commitment to that future which made sure that Marx never had to grapple with the reflexive deconstruction of everything.

But the struggle for transcendence could have another set of consequences; it could imply a different technique for the avoidance of the abyss. The progress of the will to know could be harnessed to a long term certainty through the attitude of nostalgia. Indeed, nostalgia is just as defining of modernity as the kind of relentless reflexivity and futurity which is typified in their different ways by Faustus, Faust and Karl Marx.

Both nostalgia and reflexivity suggest a transcendence of the existent and of the present which is therefore identified as a reified and as a delimiting form. The difference is that whereas reflexivity tends to push into, and thereby create, the future, nostalgia pushes into, and thereby creates, the past. Malcolm Chase and Christopher Shaw have made the important point that there is a profound connection between the utopian futurity of a Karl Marx and the sense of nostalgia. They write that 'Nostalgia becomes possible at the same time as utopia. The counterpart of the imagined future is the imagined past' (Chase and Shaw 1989: 9).

The linkage between futurity and nostalgia is worth pursuing. It can be taken as a demonstration of the possibility that the sense of nostalgia is not an ahistorical constant which is a potential feeling for any person at any time. Rather, nostalgia is only possible in certain places at certain times. In particular, Malcolm Chase and Christopher Shaw suggest that there are three prerequisites which constitute the conditions of existence for nostalgia. The point to note is that these conditions are only features of a milieu which is emerging out of the practice of the deconstruction of natural artifice. They only prevail in a context which is, therefore, able at least in principle to understand itself in its own terms.

Firstly, nostalgia can only develop in cultural circumstances where there is a notion of linear time (that is, a notion of history). The present is seen as a product of a certain past and a to be achieved future. Secondly, nostalgia requires 'some sense that the present is deficient. Most dramatically this can apply to the great declines of history, to the fall, for instance, of once great empires' (Chase and Shaw 1989: 3). It can also apply to the fall of once great interpretations of the meaning and the nature of existence with their once great fixed identities. Thirdly, nostalgia requires the existential and material presence of artifacts from the past. 'A society which simply junked all of its outworn and outmoded technology, which ruthlessly threw away ephemera and which confidently built over the developments of previous generations would lack the material objects from which nostalgia is constructed' (Chase and Shaw 1989: 4).

If these three prerequisites are pulled together, it is clear to see that nostalgia emerges in cultural circumstances in which society is seen as a milieu on the move from somewhere which is defining to somewhere else which is to be defined. In other words, nostalgia is a feature of modernity; it simultaneously provides fertile ground for certainty and deconstruction. It is one kind of response to the cultural conflict in modernity.

The importance of nostalgia to the modern imagination has also been stressed by Raymond Williams. In *The Country and the City* Williams persuasively makes the case that nostalgia is in important part a mythical response to the experience of the urban. As such, Williams argues that the *link to Jencks.* sense of futurity attaches to the city whilst the sense of nostalgia attaches to the country (Williams 1973: 297). He is in little or no doubt as to the operation of this dichotomy as a myth which helps gloss over if not wholly hide the contradictions of daily life: 'Clearly the contrast of country and city is one of the major forms in which we become conscious of a central part of our experience and of the crises of our society' (Williams 1973: 289). In other words, the country is the other of the city and, thus, constitutes a milieu of certainty in the past which is a counter-point to the sensed flux of the metropolitan present.

Williams reaches these conclusions through a study of the themes of the city and the country as they have been played out in, particularly English, literature. He believes he can identify a more or less constant harking back to some rural ideal which is typified by the certainties of definition; an ideal which almost of necessity can allow no constructive place for the modern struggle of self-definition and reflexivity (for example, witness the fate of Richardson's Clarissa; she reflexively achieves only the reification of destruction). According to Williams, the case is so obvious that 'Nostalgia, it can be said, is universal and persistent' (Williams 1973: 12).

The difficulty with Williams is that, unlike Malcolm Chase and Christopher Shaw, he fails to unpack the meanings of nostalgia. He seems to imply that it represents a more or less unitary response to the problems and contradictions of the city. Moreover, his version of historical method means that he fails to notice the essential modernity of nostalgia. Raymond Williams does not notice that nostalgia does not operate flatly as a straightforward critique of modernity. Of course, nostalgia is often harnessed to more or less accurate and telling critiques of modernity. It would be silly to pretend otherwise. But nostalgia also, and perhaps rather more interestingly, operates as a hermeneutic justification of modernity. Nostalgia posits a past which is comforting precisely because it is, and can be, no more.

The sense of nostalgia implies a double longing which revolves around a desire for something absent. Firstly, nostalgia means a certain homesickness. It presupposes that the subject of the yearning is in some way either homeless or abroad (that is, that the yearner has by accident or design found him or her self somewhere other than in the place where they think they should be. In other words, nostalgia is impossible without movement and transformation). Secondly, nostalgia implies a longing for something which is far away or of former times (the present is known to be qualitatively different to the past. In other words, in relation to the reified past the present is a reflexive achievement).

Now, in itself not unreasonably, Raymond Williams tells a tale of the latter meaning of nostalgia, but the former meaning is rather more interesting. Not least, it is only possible for me to long for home if I know that I am without my home. To be homesick requires that, firstly, I can conceive of a home in which I should dwell (I am certain) and, secondly, that I am possessed of the knowing of my homelessness. And to know that I am homeless means that I must be somewhere else other than at home. For instance, I must be in the city to know of the delights of the country, I must be in the present to know of the past or of the future. Meanwhile, for those who inhabit the found world of the country, the city beckons as the home of freedom whilst the future is a utopia in which the contradictions of the present will be resolved with the certainty of linear time (that is, the certainty of the otherwise never reached future) being guaranteed by the existence of material and imaginative artifacts from the past. This can all be interpreted as, once again, a cultural conflict between identifications of form and life, identifications of reflexivity and reification.

Consequently, nostalgia is not just a repudiation of where I am. Or, at the very least, nostalgia does not have to be only a repudiation. It is also a way of coming to terms with my present position (a way of making it my new home; I will put up pictures which remind me of the place from which I came; I will cook favourite recipes from the old country and decorate my new home in a way that my friends might consider kitsch) and of giving myself the confidence and the certainty to carry on living there (for one kind of reflection on this facet of nostalgia, see Skvorecky 1985). Nostalgia is not necessarily incompatible with the transcendence of form. Quite the contrary, it might possibly be a means of making the relentless struggle against reification even more resolute. Just like futurity, but in an admittedly different way, nostalgia gives a home and a shell of certainty to the will to know. Both futurity and nostalgia are responses to, and reflections of, the attempt to make the human sufficient unto itself.

This kind of dialectic of nostalgia is implicit to Goethe's *Faust*. Goethe shows quite clearly that nostalgia does not have to mean a kind of historical retrospection. It can also be the basis for previously unimagined exploits in the adventure of the transcendence of form. These themes are perhaps at their most pronounced towards the beginning of *Faust*. Faust's reflections on the fundamental tedium of the certainties generated by his reflexive enterprises has led him to the depths of despair. He is considering taking poison to end the seeming absurdity of it all. But Faust is called back from his contemplation on suicide by the pealing of church bells. The sound of the bells inspires a nostalgia for childhood. But the nostalgia does not lead to an escape from modernity, rather it leads to a new commitment to modernity. As Faust says, 'the sound brings back my soul's indenture / Of early years, calls me to life again' (Goethe 1949: 56). The yearning for a lost home inspires a struggle for the deliberate construction of a new and a better place in the future (and thus the present becomes doubly flawed; it is worse than the past and worse than the future).

Nostalgia means not just a long look into some halcyon past (although frequently it did and does mean precisely that). Nostalgia can also give meaning for the will to know. It can help those who are motivated by the overcoming of all forms to identify some purpose and meaning to what they are doing. Nostalgia turns the modern human lemmings away from the precipice.

The meaningfulness of nostalgia, the home it constitutes for the otherwise home-wrecking modernity, is also one of the dominant themes in the sociological narratives which ponder the possibility and implications of fixed or fluid identity. The importance of nostalgia is especially revealed in Ferdinand Tönnies' thesis of *Gesellschaft* and *Gemeinschaft*. Indeed, the kind of ideas developed by Tönnies take on a whole new resonance if they are treated as responses to the problems and possibilities of modern existence (and especially modern urban existence) rather than as more or less accurate (and therefore more or less dry) types by which the bases and implications of social relationships can be classified. Put another way, Tönnies might well be far more interesting and even entertaining than posterity would have us believe.

Tönnies was in no doubt that the distinction between Gemeinschaft and Gesellschaft operated on a number of levels. It was, of course, descriptive; it did refer to different modes of social organization and to different milieux of institutional arrangements. But the distinction was also taken to be ontological (Tönnies was very much worried by what it meant to be an individual living in each of these contexts) and historical. In other words, through this simple conceptual divide, Ferdinand Tönnies was attempting to provide some order for a whole complex web of transformations which, for him, had occurred largely within living memory. (The point of transformation within living memory might well be of immense cultural significance; unfortunately there is not the space to pursue it here. The sense of nostalgia is likely to be far stronger for those individuals and groups which have experienced radical change within their own life times. After all, it is largely impossible to make life meaningful through an emphasis on the uncertainty of everything except the certainty of uncertainty – or the uncertainty of certainty. The other question which would need to be explored is the nature and implication of the connection between personal memory and broader, societal, historical memory.)

Tönnies defined his terms very clearly. He made it plain that his book was only concerned with 'the relationships of mutual affirmation' (Tönnies 1955: 37). That is, the main concern is with how individuals live together in more or less secure social relationships. Tönnies continues: 'Every such relationship represents unity in plurality or plurality in unity. It consists of assistance, relief, services, which are transmitted back and forth from one party to another and are considered as expressions of wills and their forces' (Tönnies 1955: 37). The categories of Gemeinschaft and Gesellschaft are intended to classify the different forms of this force field which is produced in and through the relationship of wills. It is best to, once again, quote Tönnies himself. He says that 'The relationship itself, and also the resulting association, is conceived of either as real and organic life – this is the essential characteristic of the *Gemeinschaft* (community), – or as imaginary and mechanical structure – this is the concept of *Gesellschaft* (society)' (Tönnies 1955: 37).

More concretely, Gemeinschaft is strongest in the small scale and largely static rural milieu, whereas Gesellschaft is typical of the urban environment. 'Accordingly, Gemeinschaft (community) should be understood as a living organism, Gesellschaft (society) as a mechanical aggregate and artifact' (Tönnies 1955: 39). Or, put another way, Ferdinand Tönnies is identifying a milieu of life and locating it in the ostensibly genuine rural world and using it nostalgically as the counterpoint and critique of the fabricated, and therefore in some way inadequate or unsatisfactory, dwelling of the metropolis. 'The city is typical of Gesellschaft in general ... Thoughts spread and change with astonishing rapidity. Speeches and books through mass distribution become stimuli of far-reaching importance' (Tönnies 1955: 266).

As an extension of this theme, Tönnies makes it fairly plain that, for him, the relationships which typify the condition of Gemeinschaft are prior to formal reflection (and therefore beyond the bounds of the formal) whereas the relationships of Gesellschaft involve a reduction of all reflection and activities to the constraints of rational and contractual reciprocity. As such, the reciprocity and the relationships of Gemeinschaft are based on natural will whereas those of Gesellschaft involve a calculating rational will (Tönnies 1955: 38. It is worth comparing this argument with Simmel's interpretation of the impact of the money system). Quite simply and quite obviously, Tönnies is taking up the kind of mythic themes which have already been found running through the paradigmatic statements of modernity.

However, the interesting point about Tönnies' work is that even though a panic, or at least a moral concern, over the consequences of Gesellschaft is never too far away, he actually does not wish to see a universal return to Gemeinschaft. This is where his nostalgic temper becomes rather important. Tönnies' nostalgia acts precisely to recover strength and commitment to the demands of the metropolitan milieu. He wants to overcome the difficulties of Gesellschaft, not by overcoming Gesellschaft as such but by adding hermeneutic and existential certainty to it. Nostalgia is a pinch of that added ingredient of confidence.

When Tönnies talks in a nostalgic vein, he is torn between identification of a pastoral idyll and, on the contrary, identification of a tyranny of tradition. He seems to implicitly suggest that Gesellschaft is a good thing in so far as it releases the individual from the restraints of unalterable tradition (but releases the individual into what?). But it is a very bad thing in so far as it means that the individual loses all contact with the genuine and real relationships of the idyll.

Tönnies is in no doubt that Gemeinschaft gives the human a definite, bounded, secure and safe haven in the world. This is achieved because the relationships and practices of Gemeinschaft tie the individual to a very specific time and place. 'Life of the Gemeinschaft develops in permanent relation to land and homestead. It can be explained only in terms of its own existence, for its origin and, therefore, its reality are in the nature of things' (Tönnies 1955: 59). Gemeinschaft involves exactly the kind of natural artifice which modernity militantly deconstructed. The idyll might be safe and secure but it is also the most narrow bounding of humanity. Tönnies knew this well, and sees a historical process of the reification of the pastoral bliss: 'From a house which, like human beings, animals, and things, is movable, it becomes immovable like earth and soil'. He continues: 'The human being becomes bound in a twofold way, through cultivated fields and through the house in which he lives; that is to say, he is tied down by his own work' (Tönnies 1955: 58. There is more than a hint of Marx and dead labour in the final few words).

So, this nostalgia is typically modern and thoroughly ambivalent. It is predicated on the notion of linear time (Gemeinschaft and Gesellschaft are linked), and it does indeed tend to identify a time and place which has been lost. To some extent, Ferdinand Tönnies is homesick. But it is not a sickness for the bounded home of the pastoral idyll. Quite the contrary, it is a homesickness for the certainties implied by the idyll and, therefore, it is a restatement of commitment to the modern metropolis. Tönnies is trying to understand how it might be possible to provide some certainty for the individuals whose lot it is to live in the unbounded and inherently reflexive milieu of the city.

The answer is one of the reification of some forms, with the pattern and justification of the reification being legitimated by the nostalgically invoked and invented pastoral idyll of Gemeinschaft. He wants the freedom from the tyranny of tradition which is promised by Gesellschaft. But the existential consequences of that freedom can, in Tönnies' intellectual system, only be overcome by a return to the securities of Gemeinschaft. As such, the answer to the potential abyss of meaning in modernity is one of the construction of safe-houses of Gemeinschaft within a greater Gesellschaft. Tönnies does not want to give up on the modern invention of the sovereign individual, but neither does he want to see that individual flailing about in a meaningless universe.

This is a rather difficult circle to square, but square it Tönnies does. Thanks to his nostalgic temper he is able to reinvigorate existence in the city but at the price of allowing, if not actively encouraging, some new reification of form. 'Even if all controls of the Gemeinschaft are eliminated, there are nevertheless controls in the Gesellschaft to which the free and independent individuals are subject' (Tönnies 1955: 268). Here then, are the individuals who have, in fact been made sovereigns of their destinies by the overcoming and historical dissolution of the bonds of the organic links of the pastoral and the collapse of static tradition. The individual has been released into the highways and side-streets of the metropolis.

But Tönnies is worried about how those individuals will be able to live together; how they will be able to avoid falling into some kind of hermeneutic or perhaps even physical inferno. Nostalgia comes in to calm his fears; nostalgia gives Tönnies the answers. Consequently, 'For Gesellschaft ... convention takes to a large degree the place of the folkways, mores, and religion. It forbids much as detrimental to the common interest which the folkways, mores, and religion had condemned as evil in and of itself' (Tönnies 1955: 268). So, the basic question of Gesellschaft is one which is addressed to the potential fluidity of individuals. The answer is one of the linking of individuals to fixed identities which are derived from the promises of nostalgia and guaranteed by the forms of Gemeinschaft. Through nostalgia, modernity becomes inhabitable. Modernity does not have to be refused.

But for some thinkers, this turn to nostalgia was not a viable option.

For some, the modern condition was so new, so very different to everything which had preceded it, that any conception of historical linearity was quite impossible. The problems and possibilities of the modern had to be solved by modern resources alone. Any harking back to the past was nothing more than an affectation.

This is, of course, to hint at the series of assumptions which informed much of the work of Emile Durkheim. A superficial comparison might well indicate a number of very great similarities between Tönnies' division of Gemeinschaft and Gesellschaft and Durkheim's division of societal arrangements into organic and mechanical solidarity. However the surface similarities are rather deceptive. Behind them there is a complete gulf of founding suppositions. Quite simply, Durkheim's position was that a society is typified either by organic or mechanical solidarity and that it is impossible to connect the one up with the other (this is, of course, the theme of Durkheim's *The Division of Labour in Society*; see Durkheim 1984). Meanwhile Tönnies slid from the one type of social relationship to the other more or less at will. For Emile Durkheim, the modern world is the modern world and, therefore, the answers to its problems must be modern as well (for a little more on the substantive disagreements between Durkheim and Tönnies, see Giddens 1971: 226).

Whereas Tönnies was reasonably confident that, in principle at least, the abyss of meaning could be overcome for the individual through the construction of pockets of Gemeinschaft, Durkheim is not so sure. For Durkheim, the individual is always a short step away from the most annihilating meaninglessness. In the story of Ferdinand Tönnies, the individual is always going somewhere; from fixed identity, to the flux of the city to another fixed identity. This series of stages is underpinned by the identification and assumption of a linear history. What the individual was yesterday, the individual might also be tomorrow. But Durkheim's more drastically ahistorical method meant that he could not suppose that previous conditions might be rediscovered or that the future might be the source of some absolute meaning. Durkheim's work betrays little or no trace of a sustained faith in either nostalgia or futurity.

For Durkheim, we are here and here alone, and it is only from our conditions of existence in the here and now that it is possible for us to derive a meaning for the activities we do, or do not perform. Durkheim's work revolves around a polarized, rather undialectical, version of the modern conflict between reflexivity and reification. It is quite unable to pull itself out of what consequently becomes a depressing and self-defeating opposition. On the one hand, Emile Durkheim's sociology is all about the basis and the solidity of the fixed identities which bound the individual into the moral facticity of society. But on the other hand, Durkheim's method reveals the entirely social basis of morality and society. Consequently, in knowing the truth of his certainties, he actually undermines the very possibility of any certainty. For example, it is only certain that I should, say, uphold the morality of monogamous marriage if I am certain that I am here as opposed to there. In seeking to be certain of my fixed identity as a moral being I am actually having to confront the knowledge that my identity is not fixed. There is actually no reason a priori other than society itself which determines why I should be this kind of a moral being. But I know also that if I am not a constituent part of this society I might actually be nothing. Nostalgia and futurity give me nothing except invariably badly written fictions.

In Durkheim's interpretation of the modern, the human is not going from one place to another. Quite the contrary. For Durkheim the individual is either in the only possible place or the individual is out of it. And, on the outside, meaningful existence is unsustainable. Durkheim's book *Suicide* demonstrates quite clearly some of the most profound costs of living within and without the boundaries of the fabricated order called society. If the individual is too bounded, if she or he is too much of a self-centred individual, she or he might lose touch with other individuals; she or he might also become bored with everything (perhaps just like Emma Bovary). The individual who is too bounded might become an egoist and, therefore, 'since he is detached from society, it has not sufficient hold upon him to regulate him' (Durkheim 1952: 288). For this individual, if 'his desires are not usually excited, it is because in his case the life of the passions languishes, because he is wholly introverted and not attracted by the world outside' (Durkheim 1952: 288. By way of an illustration of this point, think of Huysmans' novel, *Against Nature*). Like Goethe's Faust, the bounded individual becomes so bored that suicide seems like the only viable expression of existence.

But outside of the fabricated order, in the milieu which might be the realm of unrestrained reflexivity, the situation is not much better. It is certainly different, but the end result for the individual might well be the same. The outside is the milieu of anomie. Society gives meaning and place and direction (it gives bounds), but outside is a boundless, meaningless nothing. The reflexive individual succeeds in destroying everything and anything to which it might be possible to attach some meaning and some purpose and point. Durkheim understood anomie as the product of 'the lack of collective forces at certain points in society; that is, of groups established for the regulation of social life' (Durkheim

1952: 382). Only the formal establishment of social groups can constitute the location of meaning and if the individual is not within such a group she or he is thrown back onto entirely lone resources. But they are inadequate: 'Finding there is nothing to which he can attach himself, however, the melancholy inspired by this thought can only drive him to new self-escape, thus increasing his uneasiness and discontent' (Durkheim 1952: 288. Perhaps this point can be illustrated with Huysmans' novel, *Downstream*. I know that the heroes of Huysmans' books do not actually commit suicide as such, but the temper of the books is generally illustrative of the points Durkheim is making. It might be said that the main characters commit a kind of moral and social suicide).

In many ways, Tönnies provides a fairly classic vision of what it is to be a modern individual and, ironically, Durkheim provides a series of hints which imply a kind of transcendence of the modern individuality. Because it is so desperate to see modernity on its own terms, Durkheim's work actually achieves nothing other than the deconstruction of every certainty which it otherwise seeks to establish. Durkheim is stuck in modernity; he eschews linear history and therefore can see the world only in terms of perennially apart oppositions. For Durkheim, the unflinching acceptance of modernity as the only world that can exist after natural artifice, means that the world is either/or, inside/outside, something/nothing, meaningful/meaningless. Durkheim's individuals are either one thing or they are the negation of that thing, whereas Tönnies' individuals are one thing and potentially something else as well. Put another way, the individuals and groups which occasionally punctuate the thought of Ferdinand Tönnies are like pilgrims whereas the individuals and groups implied by Durkheim, and most definitely the individuals and groups which are transcendent in relation to the reified forms of society which Durkheim identified, are more like nomads (the idea of a distinction between pilgrims and nomads is far too neat for it to have been invented by me; I owe the terms to Zygmunt Bauman).

I propose that the dominant modern understanding was one in which the individual or the social group was identified as something like a pilgrim. The point is, of course, that a pilgrim is someone who is part of a community or group of one kind or another and who is engaged in a process of historical and spatial movement. Pilgrims go from one place to another place. Moreover, their journey is meaningful; the destination provides the purpose for the march either because it contains icons of a bygone age (that is, because of the investments of nostalgia) or because it contains promises of improvement (that is, because of the investments of futurity). Pilgrims are going and getting somewhere and during the course of the pilgrimage all identities are fixed. In many ways, the classic modern pilgrim is the Revolutionary Proletariat called forth by Karl Marx. The proletariat is marching forwards into the future. The prerequisite for the interpretation of individuals and social groups as like pilgrims is a conception of linear historical time. The pilgrim can only travel because there is a direct causal connection of one kind or another between the past, the present and the future, between here and there. Similarly, therefore, the history assumed by Ferdinand Tönnies is a history of pilgrimage because it assumes connections between Gemeinschaft and Gesellschaft. Indeed, if it was not for those connections, Tönnies' interpretation of the modern would be impossible.

However, just as modern identity contained the kind of tragic core which the existentialists amongst others tried to reveal, so the pilgrim is also a tragic figure. This is because of two factors.

Firstly, the basic difficulty for the pilgrim is that the individual or group which sets out on the journey does not possess the same identity as the individual or group which arrives at the destination. Either the destination is actually pushed out of reach; it slips away at the moment when it seems closest. After all, the whole point of the future is that it is not a part of the present, and we are always in the present and, therefore, logically incapable of reaching the future. The tragedy of the future is the impossibility of the arrival of the future (this lesson was taught most profoundly by the experience of really existing socialism; it never became Communism). Or at the moment of arrival the identity of the pilgrim is transformed; the pilgrim achieves his or her purpose and thus, overcomes the former fixed identity of attempting to achieve a purpose. For example, the Revolutionary Proletariat ceases to have the identity of a class in itself and instead, becomes something quite new, a class for itself.

Secondly, and historically perhaps rather more seriously, pilgrimages have leaders and followers. Some individuals are invested with a greater access to the secrets of the journey than others to the extent that they can claim and maintain exclusive access to high status resources. Typically in most of the modern pilgrimages the intellectuals tried to claim a place at the head of the procession. The problem is that in so doing the leaders necessarily deny the self-sufficient self-definition of the led (another latent possibility within Kant's essay on Enlightenment. This problem with the pilgrimage was yet another of the lessons taught by really existing socialism). Moreover, and pragmatically perhaps just as importantly, the leaders might not be very good map-readers.

But with his complete imprisonment within modernity, Emile Durkheim ironically implies, but does not realize, a rather different kind of identity. With his dependence on irreconcilable dichotomies of the inside and the outside, Durkheim intimates a condition in which the transcendence of the form of the pilgrim involves the emergence of the reflexivity of the nomad. The possibility of the transcendence of modern forms is implied so strongly by Durkheim precisely because he can see no realistic alternative to the present arrangements, precisely because he is so scared by what might lurk out there. Durkheim's attempts to shore up the modern arrangements forced him to open up nothing but the other side of the modern. Durkheim himself saw that other side as a simple annihilation, but it might be open to interpretation in a totally different way.

The whole point of the nomad, of course, is that as an individual or a group the nomad simply travels. The journey has no point; it has no place of origin and neither, for that matter, does it have a destination. The nomad has no fixed identity, rather his or her identity is simply something which emerges out of the transient play of roles, resources and relationships. But, and as Gilles Deleuze and Felix Guattari have realized, to the extent that the travelling of the nomad has no point, and to the extent that the nomad moves in a milieu which has no boundaries and therefore no places and no directions, the nomad is historically stationary.

> The nomad distributes himself in a smooth space, he occupies, inhabits, holds that space; that is his territorial principle. It is therefore false to define the nomad by movement ... the nomad is on the contrary *he who does not move.*
>
> (Deleuze and Guattari 1986: 51)

Since the terrain of the nomad is simply the transcendence of the terrain of the pilgrim, it is imagined and called forth as flat and featureless whereas that of the pilgrim is punctuated with milestones and sacred sites. 'It is in this sense that the nomad has no points, paths or land, even though he does by all appearance' (Deleuze and Guattari 1986: 52). The nomad-like groups interpret the landscapes of social and cultural relationships as more or less quite without features. Deleuze and Guattari are not saying that the landscape really is barren; rather they are saying that it is interpreted and apprehended as if it was barren. The nomads do not understand themselves to be possessed of the ability either to identify or make the landmarks which would turn spatial and temporal movement into the travelling of a pilgrimage.

Perhaps the most significant of these nomad-like groups is, in fact, the reflexive intellectuals who have managed to deconstruct the conditions of modernity. A glimpse of the nomad-like existence can be found in the work of Theodor Adorno. For Adorno, the modern institutions and arrangements were things to be known rather than taken for granted. But in that knowing he managed to transcend the erstwhile commitment to the Great Proletarian Revolution. Similarly, the narrative of linear time lost any guarantees in the future. The past simply became the embryo form of the existing disasters. Consequently, Adorno succeeded in doing nothing other than removing himself from any sense of the going somewhere. He deconstructed and transcended the possibility that he might be the leader of the modern pilgrimage to the new and better world. Instead, all he was able to do was offer a melancholic reflection on the present. He became rather like a nomad (all of these moves are especially clear in Adorno's famous essay on jazz. See Adorno 1989).

The nomad-like condition revolves around consumption. For example, a reflexive intellectual like Theodor Adorno commenced with an attempt to produce and to write the meanings of the world for himself. But in so far as that attempt to write became a form (and indeed a formal obligation of the intellectual) so it too became something to be interrogated. In other words, the intellectual was fated to try to read the conditions of the writing of the world. The knowledge of production transcendentally became a knowledge of consumption. But this move into consumption also applies to other groups. Other nomad-like identities coalesce wherever there are possibilities for the more or less free consumption of earlier productions (or of the production carried out by others). As such, typical nomad-like identities can be seen in the various social and cultural groups which revolve around and practise primarily rituals of display (for example, various groups in the city, groups which consume similar styles of fashion) or of hermeneutic transcendence without linear time.

Some of the more significant sociological dimensions of this transformation have been drawn out by Michel Maffesoli. Maffesoli does not talk about pilgrim-like and nomad-like identities, but his work can help to clarify precisely what these types of identity involve. Instead, Maffesoli is explicitly concerned with the features of post-modernity. Like Emile Durkheim, Michel Maffesoli is concerned with the basis of social solidarity and indeed, with the destiny of society itself. Maffesoli has suggested that the fixed identities bequeathed and associated with the bounded reification called society have been overcome by the fluid and largely directionless identities of what he calls neo-tribalism and sociality (see Maffesoli 1989). Maffesoli argues that the notion of the rational sovereign individual who is the intuited centre of things has been overcome by the emergence of the deindividualized persona who is perpetually peripheral and who represents no deep truths; the persona is simply the amalgam of roles.

The post-modern persona, for Maffesoli, represents a replacement of the modern individual. The persona is perpetually playing roles on the basis of aesthetic or relational empathy with others in a pointless theatre of the world. In other words, Maffesoli seeks to draw a distinction between the imaginary abstractions of modernity and what he understands to be the more immediate and direct experiences of post-modernity. As Maffesoli writes: 'Here lies the difference between an abstractive/rational period, and an empathetic time. The former relates to the principle of individuation or separation, while the latter is dominated by indifferentiation, the "losing" of self into a collective subject'. He continues: 'This indifferentiation is what I refer to as *neo-tribalism*' (Maffesoli 1988: 145).

According to Maffesoli, these neo-tribes are embedded in the rituals and performances of daily life. Maffesoli wants to emphasize exactly the mundane and everyday activities which linear time with its obligations to the future sought to denigrate. Maffesoli stresses 'the apparently innocent gestures that constitute the life of our streets and markets, which structure that life without quality too often considered to be insignificant' (Maffesoli 1989: 6). Whereas the modern pilgrims were part of a society which escaped any empirical perception (society is nothing other than an imaginary), the neo-tribes reflect and practise a sociality which is defined precisely by its impermanence and consequently, its inability to escape the present and thus operate in terms of linear time. As Maffesoli writes, 'In effect, "presentism", . . . but emphasizing the theme that there is no need to look for another life behind whatever is given to us to see (or to live), recalls that the only reality is phenomenal' (Maffesoli 1989: 2). In these ways, then, the kinds of groupings identified by Maffesoli are not subject to movement nor indeed to any single, fixed, truth. They simply are what they are in the present. In relation to the grand projects and duties of the modern pilgrims, they are rather more like nomads.

Indeed, Maffesoli has explicitly tried to explain that the groupings which are constituted in the 'experiences of the other' which are the basis of sociality represent a transcendence of everything which the modern pilgrims were intended to be like. For example, he tries to develop something by way of an ideal type of the category of 'the people' in order to understand the extent of the experiences of others (and hence the boundaries of sociality). According to Michel Maffesoli, this 'people is a massive undefined reality. It could be characterized by amorphousness, non-action and the "non-logical"; this is in contrast, for example, to the proletariat, which corresponds to an identity (the "historical subject" in the Marxist tradition)' (Maffesoli 1989: 7). He continues to spell out the identity of the proletariat so that the radically different basis of the people constructed in and through sociality becomes clearer: 'The proletariat has an action to realize, an action which, if it is rational, is inscribed in the meaning of history' (Maffesoli 1989: 7). The people has no such action or truth to realize (clearly, there are important similarities between Maffesoli's category of the people and Baudrillard's category of the masses).

Maffesoli helps to clarify the nature of the identities and groupings which can be interpreted as typical of post-modernity. Quite simply, the modern institutions and arrangements upheld fixed identities which were guaranteed and for that matter turned into something which could be endured because they were tied to the promises of a golden future or to the memories of a safe and secure past. Consequently, these forms became reifications from the point of view of the practitioners of the culture of reflexive discourse (typically the intellectuals). Moreover, the reflexively generated identities do not involve any kind of seeking; even less do they imply the finding of some deeper reality. There is nothing to find and no definite map of the landscape which is to be searched.

Instead, the identities and perceptions of time and history which have transcended what are held to be the reifications of modernity involve a kind of retreat into the present (to recall a phrase coined by Norbert Elias). To this extent then, post-modernity is a milieu which is not so much without history but rather, a milieu which deliberately refuses to accept the perceived requirements of linear time. As such, within post-modernity nostalgia becomes nothing more than a style or a more or less revocable aesthetic choice. After all, beneath the surface of the veneer of the past, there is actually nothing out there to be nostalgic about.

Chapter 4

Technology

Pilgrims go from here to there, and it is exactly the possibility of the arrival at the place marked on the map, or at least the wager that can be placed on the likelihood of arrival, which makes the journey worthwhile and important. After all, and admittedly somewhat before the onset of the modern deconstruction of natural artifice, it was only the seeking of 'the holy blissful martyr' which meant that the pilgrims 'from every shire's end / Of England, down to Canterbury they wend' (Chaucer 1951: 19). However, with the emergence of the modern institutions, arrangements and imaginations, the purpose lent by the martyr was replaced by rather more secular ends. Max Weber demonstrated, and indeed helped to reinforce, the acknowledgement that modernity meant the disenchantment of the world and the transformation of the religiously motivated pilgrim into a traveller who was seeking a little bit of heaven here on earth (this is, of course, part of the main story of Weber's Protestant Ethic thesis; see Weber 1930).

But virtually by definition the secular heaven was something to be attained. The goal of the pilgrimage was a condition and a location of the future. The individuals of the modern arrangements were thus established as people who were obliged to go forwards if they were to stand any chance whatsoever of living in a satisfactory world. Consequently, it was frequently the case that the dream of the future could easily turn into the nightmare of the present.

The modern imagination posited an end and a guiding thread to the deconstruction of natural artifice. But the tragedy (or at least the rather unfortunate problem) of the modern was precisely the impossibility of the achievement of the future. The modern forms and arrangements justified and nurtured the most astonishing hope, and thereby justified and nurtured the most amazing efforts of societal self-definition. But the hoped for result could never be achieved. The individuals and institutions of modernity could operate on the basis of a great hope but only because in the last instance the hope was quite futile. However, the hope was so great that the modern social and cultural groups actually never had to realize the futility of their ambitions. After all, the achievement of hope meant the most determined efforts in the here and now. And staying busy is one of the best ways of keeping one's mind off niggling worries. The individuals and the groups of modernity were too busy carrying out projects of construction and deconstruction to notice that, however hard they tried, the future never seemed to get any closer.

Essentially, the modern social and cultural groups, tied as they were to their fixed and seemingly true identities, were aware that they could depart the haven of the secularized Tabard Inn, but they were never able to come to terms with the fact that Canterbury was always over the horizon (symptomatically, and perhaps even inevitably, within the text at least, Chaucer's pilgrims never get to the shrine; it remains in the future. They are always going to Canterbury. Perhaps this discussion would seem a little less metaphorical if, for Canterbury, one reads 'Communism in the Soviet Union'). Yet the pilgrims never doubted the point of their journey. They continually recommitted themselves to it either by telling themselves that with the next step the pinnacle of the spire would prick the horizon, or by telling themselves that the pleasant and nostalgically recalled past made the future utterly necessary. Either that, or they avoided the futility of it all with entertainment. Yet however the pilgrims kept up morale, the journey became more important than the arriving.

Moreover, since the point of the pilgrimage could not be found within the prevailing arrangements (if it could, a pilgrimage would be quite unnecessary; the end is already here), the confidence in the guarantees and the shape of the future had to be the possession of an exclusive elite. After all, if possession of the secrets of the future or of the truths of identity had not belonged to some special elite which guarded it very jealously and if, instead, everyone had known for sure what the future had in store, then once again, no pilgrimage would have been necessary. The ideal would have been already present within the real. Consequently, without the activity of elite groups and, more importantly, without their ability to secure widespread consent for the marches into the future, modernity would have stopped. The groups with specialist knowledge or with a claim to the secrets of history could thus become the legitimate leaders of the pilgrims. Indeed, their leadership more or less of necessity became reified. To some extent the elite groups (such as the Bolsheviks, or the nuclear scientists, or the economists) stepped onto the pedestal which had previously been the basis of God.

Precisely this paradox of the modern is reflected in Franz Kafka's very short story, 'The Problem of Our Laws' (Kafka 1979). The story is about a community which is governed by a very secretive and traditionally legitimate nobility. The nobility claims exclusive access to the knowledge of the law and its obligations. It also makes sure that all the other social groups remain ignorant of the truth of the law. Kafka's narrator of the tale says that 'Unfortunately our laws are not generally known; they are the secret of the small group of noblemen who govern us' (Kafka 1979: 128). The dominance of the nobility is accepted by 'the common people' on the grounds that tradition has established that the nobility know the secret of the law and wield it fairly and without self-interest: 'the nobles stand above the law, and that seems to be the very reason why the law has been given over exclusively to their hands' (Kafka 1979: 128). Apart from the nobility, all other social groups have axes of their own to grind; they lack the objectivity and detachment which would make them neutral arbiters of the truth. The nobility are accepted as self-evidently neutral precisely because they control the law.

In Kafka's story, then, the rule of law is taken for granted. But in practical terms that acceptance means that the rule of the nobility is pushed quite beyond question. Since the secret of the law is known only by the nobility, only they can claim to know what is to be done and indeed, what has to be done. But Kafka allows a doubt to creep in to this otherwise watertight situation. If the law is only known by the nobility, and if everyone else is necessarily ignorant of its code, then perhaps it is actually the case that the law does not exist. Perhaps the only secret is the secret that there is no secret. In other words, the arrangements described by Kafka revolve around the possibility of the most immense abyss of meaning. Kafka hints at the possibility that despite legal and ritual claims to the contrary, this world actually has no deep and inviolable structures. Unlike the pre-modern world of the ancients, it respects no absolute boundaries. Within this world there might well be nothing which can never be transgressed. Consequently, this world might actually be meaningless without the simple assumption and tradition that it is meaningful.

With this disturbing possibility, Franz Kafka goes quite a long way towards clarifying the nature of authority and meaning in the conditions of modernity. He helps to show that it is only with the greatest effort and only thanks to reification that the institutions and arrangements of modernity can hide the abyss created by deconstruction of natural artifice. Kafka helps explain why modern pilgrimages were doomed to failure at exactly the time when their achievement evidently came closest to hand.

Kafka says that the abyss of meaning is only avoided by the formal belief in the existence of the laws: 'There is a tradition that they exist and are entrusted as a secret to the nobility, but this is not and cannot be more than an ancient tradition to which age lends authority' (Kafka 1979: 128). In other words the glimpse of the abyss is avoided through the identification of a historical linearity which links the past to the future. The potential abyss in the present is avoided through a relentless recommitment to the destiny which is known only by the nobility.

Kafka writes that the situation 'so gloomy as far as the present is concerned, is lightened only by the belief that one day the time will come when both the tradition and our study of it will arrive ... at their conclusion'. He continues to describe the point of arrival. It is a condition in which the world is perfectly reflexive: 'all will have become clear ... the law will at last belong to the people, and the nobility will vanish' (Kafka 1979: 129). That is, the future is called forth and imagined as transcendent in relation to the obscurity and utterly reified relationships of the present. But Kafka unerringly spots the twist in the tail. Basically, the future in which the law is known by all and in which the nobility has quite disappeared can never arrive. The hermeneutic and the practical risks of the journey to the perfectly clear and reflexive future are so great that any arrival is quite unimaginable. It is too frightening to arrive at the goal of the pilgrimage. The future is the only thing which makes the present meaningful and thus, to achieve the future is to make the present meaningless. Kafka puts it differently: 'The one visible and indubitable law that is imposed upon us is the nobility, and could it really be our wish to deprive ourselves of this solitary law?' (Kafka 1979: 130).

In many ways, Franz Kafka's story is a very profound reflection on the problems of modernity (although of course, it also contains specifically Judaic themes). Kafka was aware that pilgrimages are posited on the actual non-arrival of the pilgrims either because they are not yet pure enough to witness the miracles ('rather are we inclined to hate ourselves because we cannot yet be judged worthy of the law' (Kafka 1979: 129)), or because the leaders who exclusively know the secrets tell the pilgrims that they are not quite good enough. Yet the pilgrims still have to assume, or they have to be told, that arrival is a realistic possibility. That is the only way the march into the future and out of the past can be given any sort of meaning and purpose. To this extent the modern pilgrimages, and most typically and obviously the great journeys into the future called Communism, are all logically absurd and utterly incapable of their achievement.

The whole point of Communism for the Communists was that it was an ideal and not at all a real condition. However, whilst the nobility of Communism (that is, most notably, the Bolsheviks and the Leninists) might not have been as disinterested in themselves as the nobility of Kafka's story, it was still the case that with their claim to the exclusive possession of the secrets of the universal human future they were able to provide some solitary hope and meaning. This was despite the inevitable tendency of the future relentlessly to slip away. Perhaps much of the talk about the end of history which emerged immediately after the collapse of Communism in Central and Eastern Europe can be taken as some kind of reflection of the problems and aporia which appear when the hope of a destiny is destroyed. In this way, then, the post-modern condition is one in which the present is the only fact; the future is beyond the knowing and the past simply becomes a reservoir for sanitized certainties or profit-making opportunities.

The modern arrangements tended towards the reification of the agents and products of the will to certainty. Moreover, they turned the will to know into the search for hidden meanings which would eventually reveal the ultimate truth. Consequently, the future which was the point of activity in the present was subjected to a kind of double propulsion into infinity. On the one hand, the future was pushed one more day away with the dawn of each new day. The costs of being deprived of the promise of the future were so great that the future could never be allowed to arrive (even if the arrival of the future had not been logically impossible). On the other hand, as the position of the modern nobility was increasingly challenged (less inflatedly; as the status and position of the intellectuals was increasingly marginalized as they were seen to cost too much and 'boil no cabbages'), the modern forms were deprived of whatever modest legality they were able to call their own. Instead, the institutions and arrangements of modernity became their own tradition; they became something like a second nature.

As such, the assumption of linear time is not just undermined by the practices and movements of transcendence. It is also simply cast aside. The connections between the past, the present and the future which are so important to the grand designs and projects of the modern forms are torn apart. Instead of being a more or less temporary halt on some greater process of progress, the present has become something in itself. Ironically, the rather bounded meanings of the modern pilgrimages implied a fairly unbounded lineage of history, whilst the unbounded meanings of the post-modern sociality (unbounded because of the transcendence of fixed identities) actually involves the bounding of the present.

In many ways, this collapse of the single narrative of modern history (a narrative with its sovereign authors, its pilgrims and its single although mysterious meaning) is the essence of the post-modern nomad-like condition. Nomads do not move in the linear time of history. Indeed, from the point of view of the modern pilgrims and pilgrimages, nomads do not move at all. The terrain of the nomads is perceived by the pilgrims and the nomads themselves as lacking certain landmarks (that is, it seems to involve no definite stages of history or civilization or progress. For the pilgrims that emptiness is due to the confusion which is perceived as the other side of the boundaries. For the nomad-like groups the emptiness is a direct consequence of the transcendence of form). Therefore it can be the basis of no meaningful spatial or temporal movement. After all, there are no fixed points which can constitute the static measure of how far the nomad-like groups have gone. Instead, the post-modern nomads are stuck in an inescapable present. They have been deprived of both the solitary law and the guaranteed meanings of the continuity of linear history.

Instead of aiming into futurity and instead of measuring the present in terms of an ideal future, the nomad-like groups simply demonstrate and practise sociality and adequacy in the here and now (so, for example, the intellectuals cease to be moral leaders and instead become problem-solvers). But, in the most profound sense, those demonstrations are quite pointless. It is as if the motley crew who met at the Tabard Inn were having such a good time, or could not imagine having a better time, that they locked the doors which would have led them to Canterbury and instead, stayed inside to get more and more drunk. Eventually they totally forgot that a world existed outside, and nobody had the nobility or could claim access to truths to make the erstwhile pilgrims remember.

Or at least, that is the promise if the nomad-like condition is interpreted simply as a hermeneutic event. But perhaps the terrain actually is not so empty. Quite the contrary, the resources of modernity which constructed and shored up the fabricated order of things indeed have a very significant legacy for post-modernity. Whilst the modern imaginations and arrangements might be susceptible to relatively easy transcendence, the same does not hold true for the modern institutions and material products. They continue long after the reason for their emergence and initial construction has disappeared (long after the secret of their particular law has been revealed). In particular, the possibility of transcendence most certainly does not hold true for modern technology.

The modern technology represented so many practical and material attempts to ensure the possibility of the building of a magnificent and self-sufficient dwelling in the world. It stepped in to the gap which appeared when the order of things could no longer be assumed to be constructed by nature. Technology is, therefore, a material proof of the connection of the human to a linear time. It makes sure that history is the story of progress. The trajectory of progress is represented for modernity in the increasing ability and interest to deconstruct natural artifice and put up a societally imposed set of meanings in its place. In other words, technology is something like the material shell and the means of propulsion of the modern pilgrim-like enterprises. The tragedy which confronts the post-modern nomad-like groups is the problem that technology continues long after its justifications and legitimations have been transcended.

For example, nuclear power stations continue even though it is impossible to believe as self-evident the legitimating narratives of the 'peaceful atom' and inexhaustible cheap electricity. Nuclear weapons go on of their own accord even though the legitimating narrative of deterrence is logically incoherent. Anthony Giddens has made the rather simple but nevertheless telling point that 'We can never be sure that deterrence "works," short of the actual occurrence of a nuclear combat – which shows that it does not' (Giddens 1990: 128). In a similar vein, Giddens goes on to suggest that 'the hypothesis of a nuclear winter will remain just that unless its actual occurrence makes any such consideration altogether irrelevant' (Giddens 1990: 128).

For the post-modern nomad-like groups, even more than for the modern pilgrims (but indeed, for them as well), technology tends to come to take on that overwhelming and independent existence which had once been attributed to God or to Nature. Technological disasters have the same resonance of force from outside which had once been invested in hurricanes or volcanoes. The technology which had been developed in an effort to establish and defend the fabricated order of modernity is, from the point of view of the post-modern, quite beyond the bounds of reflexivity. Technology confronts the post-modern as an independent system in its own right. Arguably it is not apprehended as an aspect of the societal itself. The situation can only be exacerbated by the tendency of technology to carry on into the unimaginable future whilst the nomad-like groups remain tied to the never-ending present.

The transformation of the status of technology from the apparatus of societal independence to a reification which is perceived as independent of the societal explains why it has taken on some of the qualities which were previously attributed to God or to Nature. In so far as nature can, from the point of view of modernity, be defined as that which is beyond the bounds of the societal, then from the point of view of post-modernity, technology is apprehended as having exactly the same status. Consequently, technology tends to become something which can only really be understood through narrative conventions which refer to erstwhile natural activities and events. In many ways, the situation is illustrated in the attempts which are made by the more populist technicians and broadcasters to insinuate technology in the common sense of everyday life. For example the existence of computer viruses (indeed, the very phrase 'computer viruses') is invariably explained through narratives which are obviously drawn from the milieu of cancerous diseases of the human body.

Cancer is invariably constructed as an illness about which the individual person is able to do little or nothing without the help of a battery of professional experts (and even then, the help might be too late). Cancer comes to the individual from outside, to strike him or her down in the prime of life. It frustrates the hopes of a full and rich life; cancer is interpreted and understood as the body's equivalent of the apocalyptic thunderbolts from the blue. Cancer is a piece of the filth of nature which transgresses outside of its proper boundaries illicitly to influence social relationships.

Indeed, this might help explain much of the fear of the cancerous death; death by cancer is much more frightening than the more social and cultural death by heart disease. For some heart disease can be a high status illness which attests to personal courage and the intensity of life. Cancer never does that; it is on the contrary interpreted as a simple destruction. Cancer is in many senses of the word a waste whereas heart disease is, in as many senses of the word again, an intimation of excess. As such, the former death is constructed and interpreted as far more threatening and dreadful than the latter (because the former is a natural process and the latter is a social process. Of course, for a profound analysis of the meanings of cancer it is necessary to read Susan Sontag's essay on the metaphors of illness: see Sontag 1991. Sontag also comments on the narrative construction of computer viruses and so forth).

Technological occurrences like computer viruses are narratively constructed in a way which is directly comparable to a greater or lesser degree with the construction of death by cancer. Computer viruses too arrive mysteriously to strike down systems which are constructed as able otherwise to function efficiently and with a tendency towards equilibrium. The viruses are invariably given names with slightly apocalyptic resonance; they are either a retribution from the past or tantamount to a visitation by a secularized Angel of Death. However, whilst the Angel might be secular, she is not at all disenchanted; the fairies have moved from the bottom of the back garden and into the wordprocessor.

To some extent, the possibility of the tendency towards the enchantment of the technologies which were originally such an important aspect of disenchantment was glimpsed by Max Weber. In the 'Science as a Vocation' essay, Weber made the point that motor cars have come to take on the quality of mysterious and self-animated objects which are quite independent of the driver. Unless they have special training and expertise (to recall Kafka, unless they are members of the nobility), individuals have little or no understanding of how a motor car actually works (Weber 1948: 139).

By technology, I am seeking to imply something rather more than individual machines and computers. Indeed, as a sociological category technology goes far, far beyond the relatively restricted meanings of the applied sciences. Rather, and following the useful lead of Rosalind Williams, 'technologies are best considered as environments rather than as objects' (Williams 1990: 127). According to Williams, such an environmental perspective on technology means that 'Technological change is best evaluated in terms of the general direction of change rather than in terms of the supposed effects of this or that device' (Williams 1990: 127). In other words, the actual individual piece of technological equipment is actually less interesting, and of less value as a resource for interpretation, than the general social and cultural trends and attitudes which it reveals.

Williams makes the assertion that 'Technologies cannot simply be thought of as neutral tools that are used by people who are good, or bad, or some mixture of these stable elements, and that are used for ends that are good, bad, or some mixture' (Williams 1990: 127). Her point is that technology is something approaching an all encompassing and an all inclusive environment which has a profound shaping influence on those who would shape technology itself: 'The user changes as the technological environment does' (Williams 1990: 127).

This close connection between technology and 'the user' has been demonstrated quite brilliantly by Wolfgang Schivelbusch. In two splendid and thoroughly enjoyable books he has shown how the currently rather mundane technologies of the railway and artificial light have totally transformed the possibilities and the boundaries of social and cultural activity (Schivelbusch has the rare knack of making one want to make a long railway journey). He also shows how the felt needs of social and cultural life have transformed the technologies (Wolfgang Schivelbusch is very far from being a technological determinist. See Schivelbusch 1980, 1988).

In *The Railway Journey* Schivelbusch provides an indication of how the technology of locomotive transport was, in the early nineteenth century, interpreted and understood as a special kind of environment. He illustrates the unique nature of railway technology by contrasting it with the road and canal transport which it replaced. According to Wolfgang Schivelbusch, the earlier transportation methods of roads and canals involve 'a technical and an economic distinction between the *route* and the *means* ... Route and means of transportation exist independently from one another, because individual movement of vehicles – their mutual flexibility in granting right-of-way, etc. – is technically possible' (Schivelbusch 1980:19). In other words, road and canal transport developed in the eighteenth century as systems which were not independent; they were simply a means of movement which had to be activated and employed through deliberate social and cultural activity.

But with the development of the railway, the situation is drastically changed. Railways are constructed as an independent and self-defining environment which defines activity rather than permits activity to be defining of it. Schivelbusch points out that 'Route and vehicle become technically conjoined on the railroad: there is no leeway between the rails and the vehicle running on them, nor is it possible for one train to "pull over" when confronted with another one' (Schivelbusch 1980: 19). According to this analysis then, the technology of the railway has a direct and major impact on what is done on the railway. The form becomes an end in itself. Schivelbusch continues: 'This is realized early on: all initial definitions of the railroad unanimously describe it as a machine consisting of the rails *and* of the vehicles running on them' (Schivelbusch 1980: 19–20).

The development of the railway as an environment in itself necessarily implied a tendency towards the reification of the possibilities of the technology: 'the mechanization of formerly organic motive powers by the steam engine was experienced as denaturalization and desensualization' (Schivelbusch 1980: 23). According to Schivelbusch, that sense of denaturalization was exacerbated by the tendency of railway lines to cut across the landscape in straight lines and thus be defining of the physical surroundings. Railway lines tend not to follow the lines of hills and rivers. 'The alienation from immediate, living nature that was initiated by the mechanization of motive power is increased as the railroad is constructed straight across the terrain, as if drawn with a ruler.' Consequently: 'The railroad is to the traditional highway as the steam engine is to the draft animal: in both cases, mechanical regularity triumphs over natural irregularity' (Schivelbusch 1980: 25).

In her book *Notes on the Underground*, which clearly owes debts to the temper of Schivelbusch's work if not to the detail, Rosalind Williams makes a number of broadly compatible arguments. Williams explores how images of the underground were used in nineteenth century literature. She proposes the thesis that these subterranean worlds can be read as metaphors for the emergence of the modern technological environment from which all organic life and irregularity has been ejected. The artificiality, the fabricated status, of the modern meets its counterpart in literary images of the artificial and lifeless universe below the earth. Williams writes that 'Subterranean surroundings, whether real or imaginary, furnish a model of an artificial environment from which nature has been effectively banished. Human beings who live underground must use mechanical devices to provide the necessities of life: food, light, even air' (Williams 1990: 4). Technology determines the nature and indeed the very viability of the fabricated order and world which emerges out of the practices of modernity.

Williams continues to flesh out more of the significance of the metaphor of the underground. The important thing is that these literary reflections on (or are they reflections of? Williams is a little vague here) the artificial technological environment run directly parallel with the changes in consciousness which Schivelbusch explains at least in part by reference to the emergence of the railway. Nature has ceased to be an overwhelming reality which reminds humans of their insignificance and instead, it has become nothing more than a passive, disenchanted resource. Nature is something which is simply there, waiting to be taken up. As Rosalind Williams puts it: 'Nature provides only space. The underworld setting takes to an extreme the displacement of the natural environment by a technological one. It hypothesizes human life in a manufactured world' (Williams 1990: 4).

Technology becomes a form in its own right. As such, technology is interpreted as a milieu which is quite beyond the boundaries of the properly human and reflexive (it betrays a tendency towards becoming identified as a contradiction of 'life'). It is prone to enchantment virtually in direct proportion to the disenchantment of nature. Put another way, it might be said that from the perspective of the attempts to come to terms with the technological fabrication of the modern order of things, the deconstruction of natural artifice meant at least in part the construction of technological artifice. The process was, of course, assisted in no small measure by the inherent predictability and mechanical regularity, and yet the occasionally shocking and explosive unpredictability of technological occurrences (the occasional exception of unpredictability proves the rule of the general predictability).

Perhaps this thesis goes some way towards explaining the modern morbid fascination with railway accidents. The fascination was at its highest in the late nineteenth century. It can possibly be explained in terms of a two-fold process. Firstly, railway accidents are a demonstration that whilst technology should be completely efficient, there always remains an element of doubt. Secondly, railway disasters are, in some way, an indication of the fragility of modern fabrication (a fragility which is attenuated by the fact that railway accidents tend to be more violent than, say, horse-drawn carriage accidents. Generally, they are more destructive of life and limb). The railway possesses its own ghost in its own machine. It possesses its own demon who occasionally upsets the smooth running of the modern order of things.

The railway accident throws the naturalization and the reification of the artificial railway into sharp relief. Once again, it is worth quoting Wolfgang Schivelbusch. He writes: 'If the normal functioning of the railroad is now experienced as a natural and safe process, any *sudden interruption* of that functioning (which has now become second nature) immediately reawakens the memory of the forgotten danger and potential violence' (Schivelbusch 1980: 132). The impact of the accident is all the greater as the railway is interpreted as more and more reliable: 'the more civilized the schedule and the more efficient the technology, the more catastrophic its destruction when it collapses'. After all, 'There is an exact ratio between the level of the technology with which nature is controlled, and the degree of severity of its accidents' (Schivelbusch 1980: 133). The railway accident is an indication of the capriciousness if not the tendency towards the plain incompetence and unreliability of the modern God. (A broadly similar analysis could be made of the fear surrounding the failure of electric lighting and, early in the nineteenth century before artificial light had become an entirely taken for granted fact of the metropolis, the fear of explosions at gas works; see Schivelbusch 1988.)

All of this is to concentrate on what amounts to the cultural and historical consequences of the emergence and establishment of techno-logy. But the significance of technology goes much further even than that. Technology helped to make the modern world what it was and, to the extent that technology becomes its own legitimation and its own reason for going on, so it also plays an absolutely fundamental part in making the post-modern world what it is. To this extent, perhaps one of the potentially most profound and insightful discussions of technology, and especially of modern technology, is that provided by Heidegger.

Heidegger offers a definition of technology which pays rather more attention to specific means as opposed to Rosalind Williams' emphasis on environments. According to Martin Heidegger, 'The manufacture and utilization of equipment, tools, and machines, the manufactured and used things themselves, and the needs and ends that they serve, all belong to what technology is' (Heidegger 1978: 288). In this definition, Heidegger is trying to make the point that technology is at the same time a means to an end and a human activity. These two aspects come together because technology is fundamentally a means of the achievement of the end of dwelling in the world. Here, things begin to get a little complicated.

Martin Heidegger proposes that technology is the building of dwelling. It is only because technology allows a building of dwelling that it is actually possible to live in the world. Yet, and here Heidegger makes a rather nice dialectical move, it is only possible to dwell in the world because of building in the world. So, according to Heidegger it is the lot of humanity to build its own dwelling (we have to make our own houses; nature does not supply them ready-made) and humanity dwells to the extent that it goes about building (we have built our own houses and therefore we are able to live in terms of our destiny to build).

The two activities and attitudes of building and dwelling are mutually indivisible. As Martin Heidegger says, 'all building is in itself a dwelling ... We do not dwell because we have built, but we build and have built because we dwell, that is, because we are *dwellers*' (Heidegger 1978: 326). Consequently, it is legitimate for Heidegger to say that 'Only if we are capable of dwelling, only then can we build', but it is also possible for him to say without contradiction that 'Building ... is a distinctive letting-dwell' (Heidegger 1978: 337–8).

Now, Heidegger sees all of this in very grand ontological terms. The drift of his argument is that the dialectic of building and dwelling is a problem for all people in all places at all times. Building and dwelling are the essential truth of what it means and involves to live. In a typically sweeping manner Heidegger asserts that 'Dwelling, however, is the *basic character* of Being in keeping with which mortals exist' (Heidegger 1978: 338). Furthermore, he believes that without deliberate building and dwelling, we would be utterly homeless. He suggests that this recognition of homelessness should be seized upon as an opportunity for a recommitment to the enterprise of building and to the condition of dwelling. After all, 'as soon as man *gives thought* to his homelessness, it is a misery no longer. Rightly considered and kept well in mind, it is the sole summons that *calls* mortals into their dwelling' (Heidegger 1978: 339).

This is perhaps rather too much to stomach. It takes an astonishing certainty, if not just immodesty, to make comments about the secret of all humans everywhere. Not least, it is to impose a fixed identity on all social and cultural activity. Moreover, presumably, it is to either denigrate any activity which is not easily reconcilable into the dialectic of building and dwelling or to make that dialectic so vague that it includes everything and, actually, becomes so imprecise as a category of analysis that it is next to meaningless.

However, Martin Heidegger's comments undoubtedly do contain more than a germ of insight. But to explore that possibility, it is first necessary to deflate Heidegger's rather more universal pretensions. I wish to suggest that the dialectic of building and dwelling is only applicable and only practised in those milieux which have been successfully pursuing the deconstruction of natural artifice, After all, it is only in the wake of such deconstruction that the activity of building becomes either necessary or viable (in order to replace God's House with Man's House). If it is assumed that the order of things prevails through nature, then dwelling is a self-evident and a taken for granted condition of existence. Similarly in those circumstances building has to be taken as already carried out by the supernatural agency. Moreover, any building projects carried out through social activity, or in the name of societal self-definition, would be nothing other than so many serious affronts to the natural.

However, in the wake of deconstruction, the issue of dwelling does indeed become a pressing problem. This is simply because forms and reifications have to be established which are able to more or less coherently carry out the functions which had previously been the role of the taken for granted. In the condition of modernity, what Heidegger calls dwelling becomes a pressing and an immediate issue because the meaning of dwelling can no longer be accepted as self-evident. Building is at once the possibility and the problem of the solution to the doubts surrounding dwelling (to return to Kafka's story, the edifice of the traditional authority of the nobility created the possibility of a meaningful world but at the expense of the creation of the problem of the severe restriction of reflexivity). Heidegger's tendency towards the virtual anthropologization of the problems of building and dwelling arguably represents the unthinking move of a Western European intellectual to universalize what might in fact have been purely local issues and difficulties (I am not therefore saying that building and dwelling are not universal human problems; I am simply saying that they are definitely modern problems. That might be as much as it is legitimate to say).

Perhaps Heidegger could have got himself off the hook of an illicit universalization. After all, he knew that technology was the means of building for the end of dwelling, but he also knew that there was something unique about modern technology. Heidegger was aware that there was something about the modern technology which surrounded him that made it qualitatively different from all hitherto existing technology. Heidegger did not doubt that modern technology was in fact, modern and therefore different.

Basically, the modernity of new technology consists in the attitude which is adopted towards nature. According to Heidegger, old technology was dependent on the prior activity of nature. But he claims that new technology is characterized by a more active, interventionist attitude. The modern technology makes nature work whereas the old technology was made to work by nature. For example, the sails of the old technological tool of the windmill 'are left entirely to the wind's blowing . . . the windmill does not unlock energy from the air currents in order to store it' (Heidegger 1978: 296). But the attitude 'that rules in modern technology is a challenging . . . which puts to nature the unreasonable demand that it supply energy which can be extracted and stored as such' (Heidegger 1978: 296).

In other words, modern technology sets itself upon nature to extract or to store something (typically energy) whereas the old technology simply used up that which nature gave (it is worth comparing this point with Schivelbusch's interpretation of some of the differences between road and canal transport on the one hand and rail transport on the other). With modern technology, 'the energy concealed in nature is unlocked, what is unlocked is transformed, what is transformed is stored up, what is stored up is, in turn, distributed, and what is distributed is switched about ever anew' (Heidegger 1978: 297–8). But all of that can only happen if nature is simply there, already subordinate to technology (just as trains can only move, and for that matter can only crash, if nature has already been subordinated to the requirements of the straight railway lines). It might be said that modern technology orders the meaning and the potential of nature by confining it within bounds.

Technology imposes a destiny upon nature, a destiny which is determined only by the demands of technology itself. To quote Martin Heidegger once again, modern technology has meant that: 'Everywhere everything is ordered to stand by, to be immediately on hand, indeed to stand there just so that it may be on call for a further ordering' (Heidegger 1978: 298). Nature is reduced to the status of the standing-reserve of technology. Consequently, it is utterly disenchanted and any intrinsic qualities which might have once been invested in the natural are utterly and decisively deconstructed. Modern technology requires, and makes sure, that the world loses its erstwhile immutability and independent self-sufficiency: 'Whatever stands by in the sense of a standing-reserve no longer stands over against us as object' (Heidegger 1978: 298).

By way of illustrating this rather useful idea that with modernity nature is transformed from an active force into a standing-reserve, Heidegger talks about the Rhine. For Heidegger, the problem is that a hydroelectric plant has been built on the river. He seems to be at once outraged and amazed that the river has ceased to be a magical and a poetic, an enchanted thing about which Holderlin wrote poems (and of course about which Wagner wrote opera). Heidegger is stunned that the Rhine has instead become 'an object on call for inspection by a tour group ordered there by the vacation industry' (Heidegger 1978: 297. For that sentence at least, the sneer is much the same as Adorno's). Heidegger does not really seem to know whether the building and the dwelling of the hydroelectric plant should be applauded as a demonstration of what 'mortals' can do or whether it should give rise to utter horror at their effrontery. In the end, he plumps relatively easily for outrage and horror.

For Heidegger the hydroelectric plant with its dam has made the river the standing-reserve for the unlocking and supply of energy. It has stopped the flowing river in more than just a physical sense. The Rhine has been defined by the technology of electricity production. The river is no longer defining of itself. It has been set upon by modernity. 'The hydroelectric plant is not built into the Rhine River as was the old wooden bridge that joined bank with bank for hundreds of years. Rather the river is dammed up into the power plant.' Heidegger continues to bewail the disenchantment of the Rhine: 'What the river is now, namely, a water-power supplier, derives from the essence of the power station' (Heidegger 1978: 297).

Heidegger is implying that the significance and the meanings of the Rhine have been reduced and bounded in so far as the hydroelectric plant is made the point and the purpose of the river. Indeed, Heidegger might well have added that it does not take too long before dams and reservoirs become apprehended as nature in themselves (just as a railway cutting or a computer virus comes to seem natural). Indeed, for some people (such as anglers exploiting the standing-reserve of fish) a reservoir can become more natural than nature itself. Heidegger seeks to understand this tendency of technology to reduce and restrict the meanings of things like rivers. He introduces and uses the concept of *enframing*.

According to Heidegger, enframing is the essence of modern technology. Indeed, this essence is more important than the specific forms of technology themselves (here then Heidegger has moved away from tools or factories. Instead he is seeing technology in hermeneutic terms).

He defines enframing as: 'the gathering together which belongs to that setting-upon which challenges man and puts him in position to reveal the real, in the mode of ordering, as standing-reserve' (Heidegger 1978: 305). Now it has to be admitted that as definitions go, Heidegger's definition of enframing is perhaps more than a little obscure. However, if a little time is spent unpacking it, then the importance of enframing might become rather clearer.

When he talks about enframing, Martin Heidegger is actually trying (and perhaps failing terribly) to make a fairly simple point. Enframing is an approach to the world of things which seeks to define their meaning. As such, given that enframing is an activity which has to be carried out, the subjective agent of the enframing stands as the definer and the revealer of truth in relation to the things which are thus defined and revealed. For Heidegger, 'man' stands over and above the realm of things which is enframed. Through enframing, meanings are imposed upon things, and they encourage or require 'man' to perform certain activities (for example, the Rhine is a source of hydroelectric power, therefore the river should be enframed by the power plant). Consequently, the things out there are imposed upon and reduced to the status of the standing-reserve. So, enframing is the essence of technology and also, the definition of the natural. It is about the establishment of forms and reifications.

It should be noticeable that despite his tortuous terminology, Martin Heidegger is actually developing an argument which bears extremely close comparison with the central myth of modernity. The notion of enframing can be interpreted as a reflection of specifically modern concerns and activities. Heidegger is seemingly hinting at processes of boundary drawing and imposition. The whole purpose of enframing is that the order of things has to be imposed upon an otherwise potentially recalcitrant nature. Thereafter, the natural objects have to be forced to accommodate themselves to the requirements of the boundaries; they are denied self-sufficiency. In many ways, this is a reflection of the sensation of 'without us a deluge'. The universe is construed and constructed as a milieu of bounds. Indeed, according to Heidegger the activity of building necessarily implies yet more bounds.

Without bounds dwelling is largely impossible. Heidegger suggests that 'the bridge does not first come to a location to stand in it; rather, a location comes into existence only by virtue of the bridge' (Heidegger 1978: 332). It is building which provides the locations of dwelling; it is building which creates the boundaries which allow us to know where we are and where we are going (it is building which enables us to know who we are; we are those who go across the bridge). Here, then, the intellectual concerns which run through Georg Simmel's comments on boundaries and boundary drawing can be linked with practical activities and material processes. Rather ironically, it is Heidegger who emphasizes the material basis of boundaries far more explicitly than Georg Simmel: 'The spaces through which we go daily are provided for by locations; their essence is grounded in things of the type of buildings' (Heidegger 1978: 334).

But enframing has another implication which also goes to the very heart of modernity. Through enframing, futurity is opened up and the social world is harnessed to a destiny. Put another way, the enframing which is the essence of technology plays no small part in calling individuals and groups to the fixed identities of the pilgrim-like condition. Through enframing, the social and societal is called forth as a bounded universe which is going somewhere. The point is, of course, that enframing requires and encourages a revelation (which is in fact a creation) of the truth of nature as a standing reserve. Enframing involves the development of a technology which is able to produce and implement the truth of the standing reserve. As such, it implies a series of activities which have to be done. Indeed, the end to the process of enframing consists in the complete definition and bounding of things.

Enframing requires and creates pilgrim-like identities. Heidegger, inevitably, put it all in his own inimitable way. He said that: 'The essence of technology lies in enframing. Its holding sway belongs within destining' (Heidegger 1978: 307). Destining is assumed by Heidegger to be the essence of history. It is a revealing of truth (the truth dependent on enframing) which has to be carried out through deliberate activity (Heidegger 1978: 305–6). Destining is a pilgrimage from *here* to *there*. Destining is the intimation of futurity. It means the identification and travelling of a 'way of revealing' (Heidegger 1978: 307).

However, and in a way which is typical of the pilgrimage condition, the supposed goal of the revealing defines the path which has to be taken. In other words, the movement into futurity is not a march into the unknown. Quite the contrary; it is a journey which is defined in advance. For Martin Heidegger this is part of the serious difficulty associated with technology. It defines the future and does not allow social and cultural activity to define the future for itself. In other words, the ostensibly reflexive activity of building has become the rather more reified condition of dwelling. As Heidegger writes, 'man, thus underway, is continually approaching the brink of the possibility of pursuing and pushing forward nothing but what is revealed in ordering, and of deriving his standards on that basis' (Heidegger 1978: 307).

The enframed future defines the technological present. The forms which are meant and intended to protect social and cultural self-sufficiency are reified and therefore fundamentally defining of reflexivity. But of course, any reflexivity which is defined in advance is actually not much of a reflexivity at all. Martin Heidegger spotted this difficulty and bemoaned it. Futurity, and the pilgrimage condition of the route of destining, means that any activity or way which is not acceptable from the point of view of the supposed goal has to be denied. As Heidegger says: 'Through this the other possibility is blocked, that man might be admitted more and sooner and ever more primally to the essence of what is unconcealed and to its unconcealment' (Heidegger 1978: 307). Here, Heidegger's assumption of linear time allows him to conjure up the possibility of an alternative future which is actually little more than a reflection of the idealized Black Forest. But he seems to have been far from optimistic that the alternative future was a realistic option. Technology means that too much has been defined and reified.

Despite the intellectual thrust of his reflections on technology, Martin Heidegger did not give in to a total despair. In many ways, the ability to snatch hope from the jaws of an otherwise almost complete pessimism is the best sign of the intrinsic modernity of Heidegger's thought. Heidegger's commitment to a conception of linear time and indeed the proximity of his thought to the central myth of modernity, meant that he was always able to claim some basis for the overcoming of reification (or the overcoming of, in Heidegger's own terminology, enframing). As such, he was able to intimate a transcendence of the essence of modern technology itself.

To this extent, the crucial aspect of Heidegger's thought is his contention that it is not technology itself which is dangerous and problematic. Rather Heidegger suggests that all the difficulties are attributable to the essence of technology as enframing. In other words, the problem is not the tool but the felt need and ability to use tools in the first place. Enframing is a problem precisely because it defines the meaning of the future. Consequently, enframing illicitly imposes a single definition of the destiny of social and cultural relationships. But according to Heidegger, the pilgrimage towards any single truth is an avoidance of truth as such. After all, 'Enframing blocks the shining-forth and holding sway of truth. The destining that sends into ordering is consequently the extreme danger. What is dangerous is not technology . . . The essence of technology, as a destining of revealing, is the danger' (Heidegger 1978: 309).

Enframing is such a profound danger because, eventually, it leads to the forgetting of humanity (and, therefore, to the reification of what it is to be human). Through the essence of technology, everything is interpreted simply in terms of the standing-reserve of resources which need to be, and will be, unlocked. Any other properties or qualities become simply unimportant. For Heidegger, this state of affairs is quite terrible. As the notion of the standing-reserve takes a greater and greater hold, so the meaning of what it is to be human is diminished (clearly, there are hints of the Dialectic of Enlightenment thesis about this position: see Adorno and Horkheimer 1972). According to Heidegger, as soon as 'man in the midst of objectlessness is nothing but the orderer of the standing-reserve, then he comes to the very brink of a precipitous fall'. In that fall, man 'comes to the point where he himself will have to be taken as standing-reserve' (Heidegger 1978: 308). The tragedy is that the danger is not generally seen because man has the arrogance to tell himself that he is the master of the earth. For Heidegger, such an arrogant and conceited claim to dominion is nothing other than the most telling proof of quite how far man has fallen into the abyss of complete and inescapable reification.

Yet in commenting about the overwhelming danger which is located in the essence of technology, Heidegger is of course actually transcending it. The very act of talking about the implications of enframing means that it is to some extent possible to invoke the possibility of an absence or a collapse of enframing (and therefore an absence or a collapse of futurity as destining). But if that transcendence is not itself to become the basis of a new enframing, its essence cannot be spoken.

The very vagueness of what lies beyond the bounds of the modern is in the last instance the only hope for an escape from the reifications and reductions of modernity. This is the chance which Martin Heidegger seized. But he seized it in a manner which rather served to reinforce any claims to leadership that the intellectuals (with their culture of reflexive discourse) might wish to make. Heidegger's argument seems to be that since the modern enframing placed a great deal of emphasis on practical, material activity, so the transcendence of enframing will, or at least ought to, place a similarly great emphasis on thought.

According to Heidegger, the ambiguity at the centre of enframing is the difficulty that the technique requires the continuation of the existence of man (because man is the agent of enframing and, therefore, initially at least to some extent without the bounds of the enframed). It 'lets man endure – as yet inexperienced, but perhaps more experienced in the future – that he may be the one who is needed and used for the safekeeping of the essence of truth' (Heidegger 1978: 314). A little later, he comments that whilst the danger of enframing can never be entirely and conclusively defeated, to know of the danger is, in some small way, to overcome it: 'Human activity can never directly counter this danger . . . But human reflection can ponder the fact that all saving power must be of a higher essence than what is endangered, though at the same time kindred to it' (Heidegger 1978: 315). All of this is a possibility if we refuse to let ourselves be blinded by the marvels and horrors of technological gadgetry and, instead, attempt to unravel the hermeneutic and material essence of technology. Such an enterprise of the thinking of technology will lead to the overcoming of enframing and, quite possibly, even to the re-enchantment of entities such as the Rhine.

Now, there is no need to agree with Heidegger's conclusions, nor indeed with the disdain for technology which is so typical of the modern intellectual, to suggest that there is much of use in his thought. Because Martin Heidegger is so profoundly worried and angered by technology, he offers a sustained and a serious philosophical assault on it. But if Heidegger's work is read as philosophy alone it loses much of its resonance as myth. It certainly loses the intimations of a condition beyond the bounds of reification and the pilgrim-like condition.

Essentially, Heidegger is trying to rescue the chance for a self-defining humanity from out of the imposed destinies associated with technology. As such, on the other side of enframing and on the other side of destiny (and therefore on the other side of the pilgrimage type activities), there is simply negation. Heidegger can intimate the condition without the bounds of enframing, but he is quite unable to give it much by way of detail. All he can say is that it will have something to do with an aesthetic challenge to the essence of technology. Art can play a major part in the deconstruction and the overcoming of the profound danger associated with enframing because it is 'on the one hand, akin to the essence of technology and, on the other hand, fundamentally different from it' (Heidegger 1978: 317). Quite what this means is not readily apparent.

Arguably then, Martin Heidegger's thought does intimate the emergence of the nomad-like condition. This is because Heidegger is basically so concerned to confront and challenge the fixed identity of the pilgrim-like condition which can be seen as going hand in hand with the technique of enframing (of course, I am aware that here I have read Heidegger's concerns in terms of my own vocabulary). Heidegger achieves this through a hermeneutic assault on the essence of technology which is, in many ways, quite brilliant.

But when all is said and done the attack is only partially successful. Certainly, Heidegger is able to imply the possibility of an overcoming of the essence of technology. But technology itself remains rather untouched by all of this. Heidegger might well manage to demolish the intellectual and hermeneutic legitimations for technology but about the actual material presence of buildings and machines he manages to do absolutely nothing. As such, instead of pulling technology as a material activity within the orbit of reflexivity, he is actually pushing it way beyond any meaningful deconstruction. In Heidegger's thought, technology continues on its own merry way even though the ability to make sense of it, and indeed, even though the desire to make sense of it, has long since vanished. Consequently, to this extent the terrain of post-modernity is littered with fabricated dwellings which can only be interpreted as prisons rather than as homes. Precisely thanks to his deep desire to make the human at home in the modern world, Martin Heidegger succeeds in making it (us) even more decisively homeless.

For the post-modern condition, then, technology is confronted as an almost absolutely reified form. It is apprehended as largely impervious to any outside intervention. Since the reflexive intellectuals like Heidegger had succeeded in deconstructing the point and the purpose of technology, so they also managed to make it impossible to actually say or do anything about technology from the outside. Technology has become its own legitimating narrative. It might even be said that from the point of view of post-modernity, technology goes on simply because technology goes on. Technology is a circular and a self-referential discourse which carries on regardless of external debates (even if funding is cut, the scientists simply decamp to another place where funding is better). Technology has indeed been reified.

Ironically, the reification of the form of technology is in large part attributable to the reflexive deconstruction of the futurity which technology was intended to build and guarantee. Put another way, the operation of the will to know has meant nothing other than the ultimate inability to know anything about technology. On the one hand, the will to know has led to deconstructive hopes being placed in those properties and qualities of things which are said to lie beyond the boundaries of technological rationality (and, therefore, that which has been enframed is left largely untouched; it is simply interpreted differently. That which is without enframing is consequently prone to spiritual and mystical constructions). On the other hand, the secret of the laws of technology has been revealed to be empty. Therefore, the narratives of progress and so forth have lost much of their validity. But still technology continues. Certainly, the essence of technology is now known, but the continuation of that knowing requires the continuation of technology. Heidegger actually needed a hydroelectric plant on the Rhine (and had it not existed he would have simply found something else to moan about).

Technology, the great product of modernity, is then the site and occasion of utterly contradictory relationships and interpretations. The contradictions are the basis of the centrality of technology in the post-modern condition; it explains why the otherwise nomad-like groups do indeed tend to come up against material landmarks with some frequency. The problem is that these landmarks appear to be houses for the future, but the way in to their safe certainties cannot be found. There is no longer any way into the world of technology for those who are presently outside. For them, technology is a blind irradiating monolith rather than a possible guarantee of security.

Indeed, much of the excitement of Wolfgang Schivelbusch's work is due to the fact that he reveals the profoundly fabricated status of what is all too often taken for granted. For example, Schivelbusch inspires a wholly new interpretation of the urban environment when he points out that to an important extent the form of the metropolis was reified in the nineteenth century by the demands of centralized gas supply. Schivelbusch suggests that like the railway, the central gas supply meant the definition and delimitation in advance of what could be done: 'Once a house was connected to a central gas supply, its autonomy was over . . . No longer self-sufficiently producing its own heat and light, each house was inextricably tied to an industrial energy producer' (Schivelbusch 1988: 28). So, Wolfgang Schivelbusch has brilliantly deconstructed the virtually natural obviousness of the gas mains, and he has overcome the essence of this technology. But still the technology remains. The material technology of gas mains are themselves left untouched.

From the point of view of the post-modern, then, technology inspires one (or sometimes a combination) of three attitudes. Firstly, it is a complete reification which stands apart from social and cultural interference. Secondly, it is just too horrible to be allowed to continue. Thirdly, technology is simply unsayable; it continues but without a purpose, without any discursive legitimacy (that is, it becomes somewhat 'implosive' in Jean Baudrillard's sense of the term; see Baudrillard 1983). The technology which played such a crucial role in the fabrication of the modern human dwelling has become the second natural artifice. It has become a reification in its own right and, consequently, a major obstacle to the social and cultural self-definition which it was meant to protect and enhance. In other words, technology itself has become something which is perceived as standing in need of transcendence or deconstruction.

Chapter 5

Responsibility

Even the quickest survey of the history of social and cultural attitudes towards technology and the constructions of it reveals a very deep and serious tension. Indeed, to a very considerable extent the tension can be understood easily and fairly as yet another dimension of the dialectic between reification and reflexivity. I have of course been pursuing the thought that the perception and the identification of this dialectic is one of the key myths of European modernity and, therefore, the basic terrain of the intimation of the post-modern condition.

On the one hand, technology was accepted if not enthusiastically applauded. This was because it was identified with the material resources and guarantees of the ever better modern production and fabrication of an order of things. It offered certainties and security in the world which emerged out of the deconstruction of natural artifice. However and on the other hand, technology was just as often, if not more often, identified as actually or potentially quite terrible. According to this perspective, it might well have been the case that technology constituted the resources of societal self-sufficiency. But it was contended, these resources tended to themselves take over the meanings and the possibilities of the social life. The point to note is that neither of these attitudes or interpretations can be said to represent the definitively true or proper reading of the impact and significance of technology. Quite simply, they are both attempts to come to terms with the problems and possibilities which modernity involved. The one interpretation is, in itself, just as valid as the other.

In other words, it seems to be perfectly possible to identify the emergence and the playing out of something by way of a 'dialectic of technology' within the condition and the arrangements of modernity. Each of the interpretations of technology goes hand in hand with the other. They lend each other a content, a purpose and importantly, a perceived counter-factual condition which seemingly demonstrates the rightness of the chosen attitude. The truth content of the counter-factual was simply taken to be located in its opposition to what was interpreted as the falsity of the prevailing fact. For example, technology can be vilified on the grounds of its horrific effects on the self-defining dimensions of life. Meanwhile any effort of self-definition can be dismissed on the grounds of its incompatibility with the construction of a standing-reserve which silently waits for animation by the defining resources of technology. Each interpretation finds its justification and replenishes its energies through a simple strategy of the turning around of everything which is said in the name and interest of the other interpretation.

Indeed, without a recognition of the dialectical interweaving of the interpretations of technology, any account of its social and cultural history will only tell one side of a far more diverse story. Or at least, that is how the situation seems from the point of view of a post-modern examination of the arrangements of modernity. However, within the modern forms themselves, largely one-dimensional views were indeed frequently invested with the ability to say more or less everything which needed to be said about the social and societal implications of technology. What I am calling the dialectic of technology (which is, of course, a dialectic of interpretations rather than of actual material activities as such) can, perhaps, only be constructed from the point of view of the occupation of post-modern spaces.

The dialectic is expressed very vividly in the different accounts of industry, and what was frequently called 'manufacture', which appeared during the nineteenth century. An admiration of industry goes side by side with a distrust and condemnation of it. By 'industry' I simply mean the enterprises of productive manufacturing. In other words therefore, industry and industrialism can be accurately understood as the social organization and application of the resources associated with technology.

A concentration on industry runs through the attempts to appreciate the implications and consequences of technology. Perhaps this is not too surprising. After all, industry involves the creation of material goods and tools of self-sufficient self-definition and production in much the same way as modernity involved primarily the construction of largely hermeneutic and institutional goods and tools. Industry was a practical reflection of the ability of the modern social relationships to make the world for themselves and turn the passive standing-reserve of the things 'out there' to entirely social and cultural purposes. It was in many ways a practical demonstration of the modern hermeneutic. The modern industry and the modern hermeneutic both stressed production as opposed to consumption.

Industry and manufacture were frequently and importantly interpreted as the practical means by which the things of the world could be, and of course actually were, defined by the social rather than left to be self-defining. As Andrew Ure put the matter in *The Philosophy of Manufacture* in 1835, 'The end of manufacture is to modify the texture, form, or composition of natural objects by mechanical or chemical forces, acting either separately, combined, or in succession' (Ure 1968: 270).

Earlier, in his *Catéchisme des Industriels* of 1823–6, Saint-Simon had defined the ostensible agent of industry, the industrialist, as 'a man who works to produce, or who puts within the reach of different members of society, one or more of the material means of satisfying their needs or their physical tastes' (Saint-Simon 1976: 182). For Saint-Simon, then, industry offers the chance of an effective and reproducible escape from the reifications of anthropological needs. It also promises an escape from the no less defining compulsions of culturally constructed tastes.

It is also noticeable from the way that Saint-Simon talks about his class of the industrialists that it includes workers and owners (in a different vocabulary, proletarians and bourgeois) alike. For Saint-Simon, the fact of the matter was that the individual either was involved in industrial production or the individual was not. And all of those who were involved could be understood in much the same way; no attention had to be paid to their different relationships to industry. Indeed, Saint-Simon's industrialists actually seem to be little more than artisans writ large: 'a cartwright, a blacksmith, a locksmith, a joiner is an industrialist; a shoe-maker, a hat-maker, a linen-maker, a maker of cloth, a maker of cashmere are also industrialists; merchants, hauliers, merchant-seamen, are industrialists' (Saint-Simon 1976: 182). It must be said that, given the amazing diversity of the industrialists, one wonders if the class as identified by Saint-Simon actually means very much at all.

A protagonist of modernity like an Andrew Ure could see industry and manufacture as the source of everything which was needed in the world. Even a self-consciously radical intellectual like Henri de Saint-Simon could applaud it with scarcely a hesitation. For example, Andrew Ure was perfectly happy to talk in terms of 'The blessings which physico-mechanical science has bestowed on society, and the means it has still in store for ameliorating the lot of mankind' (Ure 1968: 273). Clearly Ure is quite sure that 'physico-mechanical science' is the motor of a linear time which is always improving.

Andrew Ure explained that industry could help humanity because it represented the construction of the means by which men and women would be released from the reification of hard labour and drudgery. Ure says with an unabashed and innocent kind of confidence in history that 'The constant aim and effect of scientific improvement in manufactures are philanthropic'. Ure goes on to detail the philanthropy of technical improvements: 'they tend to relieve the workman either from niceties of adjustment which exhaust his mind and fatigue his eyes, or from painful repetition of effort which distort or wear out his frame' (Ure 1968: 274). Here then is a statement from the period of enthusiasm for industry. At the time Ure was writing, industry and technology had already achieved a great deal; they had already played a massive part in allowing material circumstances in Western Europe, in principle at least, to meet the demands of the deconstruction of natural artifice. Basically, Ure is saying that there is little or no realistic excuse for industry not to continue providing the shell in which the societal can be defining of itself and, for that matter, separate itself more and more definitely from the passive stuff of nature.

Saint-Simon had already told a similar story about industry (and remember for these purposes, industry can be understood as a specific branch and application of the broader technology; the discussion has moved from the kinds of general philosophical concerns expressed by Martin Heidegger to a more explicitly sociological terrain). Basically, Saint-Simon's argument and radicalism was predicated on the assumption that industry represents the most efficient and rational form of production. He was consequently convinced that the industrialists should be elevated to the position of social and societal power. Moreover, the interdependencies (what Michel Maffesoli would much later call the 'experiences of others') which industry requires are held by Saint-Simon to be an intimation of the destiny of humanity. As such, the relationships and institutions associated with industry are nothing more than expressions of the universal future of humanity. Put another way, Saint-Simon is also suggesting that industry is something like the motor of linear time; it pulls humanity out of the less good past and projects humanity into the even better future. After all, 'the human race was destined to become enlightened, to refine itself by trade, to acquire the taste for work and production and then to propose the common interest as the basis for its organization' (Saint-Simon 1976: 202).

For Saint-Simon, the problem which confronts this historical destiny of the increasing societal production of itself is the continued existence of the now obsolete feudal institutions and arrangements. Saint-Simon preaches a revolutionary message which asserts that all the traditional forms, that is to say all the instances of the tendency towards second nature, should be swept away so that the emergent industrial society can be defining of itself. The period of the collapse of the old system and the establishment of the new one is a period of crisis. In 1821, Saint-Simon wrote that 'The root cause of the crisis in which the body politic has been involved for the last thirty years is the complete change in the social system'. He continues, 'the crisis essentially is the passage from a feudal ecclesiastical system to an industrial scientific one. Inevitably, it will last until the new system is fully operative' (Saint-Simon 1976: 153). This passage owes quite a lot to Comte.

In Saint-Simon's analysis, the new system will be dominant when the industrialists have gained a hold on power and leadership in much the same way as the aristocracy and the clergy had held the reins of the old order. The industrialists are ready, willing and able to take on the burden of the leadership of the process of civilization. After all, 'the masses of men organized among themselves in the industrial and scientific system possess to a high degree all the real superiority over their adversaries' (Saint-Simon 1976: 180). They are more numerous, physically stronger, richer, more rational, more moral and not least, just more intelligent. Given these many and profound advantages which the industrialists enjoy over the inhabitants of the reified arrangements, Saint-Simon thought it contrary 'to the nature of things that this weak and parasitical residue [of "the other classes of the population"] should any longer keep the leadership of a society with which it has nothing in common' (Saint-Simon 1976: 180).

In the work of Saint-Simon then, it is very easy to find a very one-dimensional view of industry and the effects it is perceived as having on social and cultural arrangements. Quite simply, for Saint-Simon, industry is in the van of the linear process of civilization. Therefore, for him the class of the industrialists can stake a legitimate claim to the possession of the driving seat of progress. Saint-Simon says little or nothing about any bad consequences that industry and technology might have. His commitment to the narrative of civilization as like a pilgrimage means that even if there are any ill effects in the short term (but there probably will not be) they are more than compensated for in the long term. For Saint-Simon, industry is a very good thing indeed and the only problems associated with it are not its fault at all. Rather, the blame for the crises which were perceived as going hand in hand with industry was laid firmly in the lap of the out of date and taken for granted old ways.

Perhaps because he wrote with a little more experience of the impact of industry, Andrew Ure was not quite as sure as Saint-Simon. Ure might well have been an innocent abroad in history, but at least he was prepared to hint that industry might possibly have some unforeseen and undesirable side-effects. The point is however, that Ure still remained tied to a one-dimensional view of technology. As such, his doubts were more or less quickly shrugged off. Ure recognized the tendency of technology to replace the human worker and indeed, to reduce the worker to the status of a mere watcher of some independent process of manufacture. But this recognition, which could have been made into a parable of terrible reification and dehumanization, was made by Ure into a tale of freedom. For Ure, the moral of the story seems to be that the worker who simply watches is therefore free to do other things whereas the worker who actually makes is tied to a single place and activity. Indeed for Ure, the development of industry has meant the emancipation of the worker from the tyranny of the kind of pre-mechanical division of labour which Adam Smith described in his famous story of pin-making.

In Smith's account of the pre-industrial division of labour, which Ure takes to be a description of actual production processes, one worker pulled the wire to make the pin, another shaped the head of the pin, and yet another shaped the point of the wire. Each worker had a separate task which was repeated over and over again. According to Ure, such production has the most awful human costs. It virtually destroys the autonomy of the worker. 'To one unvaried operation, which required unremitting dexterity and diligence, his hand and eye were constantly on the strain, or if they were suffered to swerve from their task for a time, considerable loss ensued' (Ure 1968: 281).

Machines have changed all of that. According to Ure they have made the worker free. After all, thanks to technology 'the operative needs to call his faculties only into agreeable exercise; he is seldom harassed with anxiety or fatigue, and may find many leisure moments for either amusement or meditation, without detriment to his master's interests or his own' (Ure 1968: 281). Now, Ure's argument might well cause a few raised eyebrows (but are they only raised because we read after Marx whereas Ure wrote before Marx?), but he was able to provide anecdotal evidence to support his claims. As Ure said, 'How superior in vigour and intelligence are the factory mechanics in Lancashire . . . to the handicraft artisans of London' (Ure 1968: 282). The mechanized Lancashire workers are so much fitter and healthier than their artisan London counterparts because 'The one set is familiar with almost every physico-mechanical combination, while the other seldom knows anything beyond the pin-head sphere of his daily task' (Ure 1968: 282).

Whilst Andrew Ure's work provides a hint of a dialectical interpretation of the social and cultural significance of technology, the hint is never fully realized. Ure thought that the removal of production from the sphere of active intervention on the part of the worker meant that the worker was consequently left free to do whatever she or he wanted. For Ure, the body might have been standing beside the machine and the eyes might have been watching it, but the mind was free to roam throughout a universe of its own creation. Ure's commitment to a linear history of progress and civilization, with industry as its material condition and guarantee, meant that he simply did not need to appreciate the possibility that the physically passive worker is in fact, a standing-reserve (the worker only needs to actually work if the machine breaks down; the worker waits to work whilst the machine does work).

A far more rounded and two-dimensional interpretation of technology and specifically industry (that is, technology socially organized for manufacture) is of course, to be found in the work of Karl Marx. Notwithstanding the brilliance of his understanding of the modernity which he lived, and therefore notwithstanding his overall centrality for any attempt to understand the modern, Marx is quite fascinating in this instance because of the ambivalence contained in his writing. On the one hand, Marx is quite astonished by what modern industry can achieve. He applauds its accomplishments. But, on the other hand, he is absolutely outraged by the demands which an increasingly reified manufacture places on human reflexivity. In other words, Marx provides a very clear expression of the dialectic of technology.

According to Marx, with the capitalist organization and establishment of industry, the bourgeoisie has managed to put all the previous achievements of social and cultural activity quite into the shade. In a memorable passage in *The Communist Manifesto*, Marx and Engels (although more probably just Marx; the passage bears all the hallmarks of Marx at his finest) wrote about the achievements of the bourgeoisie and of capitalist production: 'It has accomplished wonders far surpassing Egyptian pyramids, Roman aqueducts, and Gothic cathedrals; it has conducted expeditions that put in the shade all former Exoduses of nations and crusades' (Marx and Engels 1967: 83). A page or so later, Marx and Engels once again trumpet the achievements of the modern bourgeoisie and the resources it can control and conjure forth: 'The bourgeoisie, during its rule of scarce one hundred years, has created more massive and more colossal productive forces than have all preceding generations together'. They then ask a question to which any answer is quite superfluous: 'what earlier century had even a presentiment that such productive forces slumbered in the lap of social labour?' (Marx and Engels 1967: 85).

So far, Marx and Engels are rather like Saint-Simon with a more polished prose style. So far, there is nothing here which does not rest extremely easily with the most laudatory interpretations of technology. But of course, Marx (and Engels) never lost sight of the social and cultural implications of these wonders. Certainly Marx knew that if all of this had been achieved, something somewhere must have suffered. And of course, what had suffered was the humanity of the achievers; the humanity of the proletariat. For Marx, it was only possible to make the pyramids look trifling if the resources and techniques of industry and manufacture had been elevated over and above the worker to such an extent that the human was entirely denied any creativity of its own. Unlike Andrew Ure, Marx and Engels realized that the worker in Lancashire, or indeed anywhere else in the capitalist world for that matter, is not free to roam throughout the universe of the mind. The machines are so noisy that thinking is impossible. Instead, the worker is thoroughly and irrevocably passive. There is not a spark of humanity anywhere.

Marx provided a sustained account of the dark side of the impact of technological means of manufacture in Part Four of the first volume of *Capital*. For Andrew Ure, if the machine did all the work, then the worker was free to do other things, but Marx interpreted the same situation very differently indeed. According to him, if the machine did all the work, the worker was simply free to starve: 'The instrument of labour, when it takes the form of a machine, immediately becomes a competitor of the work-man himself'. Indeed, 'The self-expansion of capital by means of machinery is ... directly proportional to the number of the workpeople, whose means of livelihood have been destroyed by that machinery' (Marx 1938: 430–1). So, where Saint-Simon and Ure shared common ground in that they both asserted that industry of whatever sort meant that humanity was emancipated from the reification of anthropological needs, Marx reverses the perspective. Instead, he contends that with the capitalist organization of industry, humanity is in fact, thrown back onto the reified terrain of simple existence. For Marx, it was incontrovertibly the case that 'The instrument of labour strikes down the labourer' (Marx 1938: 432).

According to the dialectical interpretation of technology which Marx provides, and despite the fact that technology has indeed achieved a very great deal, the achievement does not mean that humanity has been raised to new heights of self-definition, reflexivity and society. Quite the contrary; in many ways the extent of the achievement is a fine measure of quite how far humanity, and especially of course the proletariat ('the class of modern wage-labourers'; Marx and Engels 1967: 79) has sunk into a pit of ossification, reification and definition from outside.

Capitalism strikes down the labourer to such an extent that as a human being, the labourer more or less completely disappears. All that remains is the ontological and frequently the physical shell of an animal (here, the philosophical discussion of 1844 re-emerges in a reflection on the practices of the 'real world'). For example, Marx proposes that in the textile industry there is a prime example of the effects of the liberation which people like Andrew Ure wrote about so enthusiastically. As Marx saw it, 'the mass of cheap human material' required by the Lancashire mills 'is composed of the individuals "liberated" by mechanical industry and improved agriculture'. The newly free workers received wages which were, according to Marx, 'no more than requisite for a miserable vege-tation, and to the extension of working time up to the maximum endurable by the human organism' (Marx 1938: 475).

Even capitalism cannot go further than the barriers which are imposed by the physical limitations of the worker. Or at least, it cannot go further unless a new piece of technology is brought into play. In *Capital*, Karl Marx argues that when the condition of the worker has been forcibly reduced to the level of 'natural obstacles that cannot be overstepped' (Marx 1938: 474), then the cycle of reification is given a further twist. The animalized workers are already reified to the extent that their ontological humanity has been undermined and they have been reduced to the level of the struggle to satisfy simple anthropological need. But even then reification can be attenuated through the use of technology to replace human activity. The definition of the worker through the devastation of all the abilities of self-definition is by no means the end of the story of entrapment: 'So soon as this point is at last reached – and it takes many years – the hour has struck for the introduction of machinery' and, in particular, the time has arrived for the development of the factory system (Marx 1938: 474).

To some extent, Marx sees the impact of the factories in a manner which is not too dissimilar to Andrew Ure. The difference is that whereas Ure drew out of the story a fairly one-dimensional moral of liberation from physical labour, Marx draws a far more dialectical and two-dimensional moral of the marginalization of human reflexivity. After all, Ure could have written the comment of Marx that: 'Modern Industry . . . sweeps away by technical means the manufacturing division of labour, under which each man is bound hand and foot for life to a single detail-operation' (Marx 1938: 489). But Ure could not and would not have continued with the observation that 'the capitalistic form of that industry reproduces this same division of labour in a still more monstrous shape; in the factory proper, by converting the workman into a living appendage of the machine' (Marx 1938: 489). A little later in *Capital*, Karl Marx asserts that industry has terrible consequences for the worker because it 'constantly threatens, by taking away the instruments of labour, to snatch from his hands his means of subsistence, and by suppressing his detail-function, to make him superfluous' (Marx 1938: 493). Hence, quite simply, the conflict and antagonism between the interests of the capitalist modern industry and the human workers.

But even Marx, with his so modern commitment to the social production of an ever better societal milieu (and with his commitment to the notion of industry as the material resource of that production), could not bring himself to throw out the baby with the bath water. Marx's rejection of the prevailing institutions and arrangements of technology by no means led to a rejection of technology as such. Quite the contrary. Despite his moral outrage and contempt for the consequences of industry and of course capitalism, Marx could still see some future good coming out of the social employment of machinery. After all, and just like Ure once again but also now a little like Saint-Simon, for Karl Marx modern industry demands the replacement of 'the detail-worker of today, crippled by life-long repetition of one and the same trivial operation, and thus reduced to the mere fragment of a man, by the fully developed individual' (Marx 1938: 494). This new individual will emerge out of the husk of the alienated and dehumanized worker of the present. A process of metamorphosis is identified as also involving something like an ontological, moral and societal pilgrimage into the clear and beautiful future.

The new model worker will be the mirror opposite of the present degraded labourer (and hence the future form represents an image of freedom in relation to the prevailing forms simply because it represents the possibility of an alternative). Marx writes that the future worker is a person 'fit for a variety of labours, ready to face any change of production, and to whom the different social functions he performs, are so many modes of giving free scope to his own natural and acquired powers' (Marx 1938: 494).

However, even though the rounded and fully human worker will appear in the Communist society of the future, it is worth noting that Marx is rather ambivalent as to how and by what the future will be generated. Of course, essays like *The Communist Manifesto* imply a degree of revolutionary voluntarism assuming that conditions are right for a revolution (that is, the proletariat actively carries out revolution but it has to be in the objective circumstances for revolution to impinge upon consciousness). Meanwhile, in the passage about the production of the new model workers, Marx seems to be saying that such a human can only appear through the compulsions of modern industry. In other words, the dialectic of technology comes to the fore once again; technology is ultimately interpreted as defining of the human rather than as defined by the human. Consequently, it is technology in its capitalist industrial form which is the source of explanation; it is reified. It is perhaps the measure of the genius of Karl Marx that he managed to pull all of these divergent perspectives into the frame of a single and more or less coherent interpretation of modernity.

For Marx then, technology and its specific social form of capitalist industrial production might well lead to the appearance of material wonders which decorate the world in new and fabulous ways. But according to Marx, the ever greater sophistication or beauty of the decorations goes hand in hand with a dilution of the qualities, potential and indeed the nature of the inhabitants. Put another way, the very fact that the modern industry can put the ancient pyramids rather into the shade can be taken to be a more or less accurate proof of quite how far capitalism and technology have gone in the dehumanization of humanity. Certainly, Karl Marx is prepared to admit the creativity and brilliance of the industrial system. But whereas Andrew Ure or Saint-Simon would have taken those marvellous productions as so many signs of civilization and progress, Marx interprets them very differently. For him they are so many signs of reification and ossification. Marx sees them as demonstrations of the establishment of definitions over the potential and possibility of self-definition.

Marx is approaching the idea that technology becomes, or has become, an end in itself. Technology can no longer be understood accurately as the material production of an ever better order of things in the modern world. It does not produce an order which protects individuals from the abyss outside, and which allows them to be defining of themselves. Technology is no longer necessarily a means to assist the journey into the future, or at least out of the past. Rather, technology is interpreted even by Marx as something which defines what the modern order of things should be like. There is little or no reasonable possibility of the rediscovery of the social and the cultural ability to be defining of technology.

Basically, the dilemma and paradox was that technology was identified and perceived as originally the best means of the attainment of the end of civilization and improvement. However, it did not take too much for the erstwhile ends to become forgotten or indeed deliberately subordinated to the means of technology in itself. Ironically, this very process of the establishment of a reified technology over and above the social and cultural ends which it was meant to secure was helped along in no small part by the efforts of the reflexive intellectuals. The point is, of course, that the modern intellectuals could only deconstruct the activity and the purpose of technology; in many ways they were quite incapable of accepting it.

Simply, technology can only continue as a socially and culturally legitimated activity on the basis of a double assumption. Firstly, the ability of technology to achieve the ostensible purpose of its employment must be beyond doubt (such that any failures are the fault of this particular machine rather than of all machines everywhere, for all time). Secondly, technology is only possible if it is assumed that there will be some moment when all the striving will be consummated and the glories of the technological enterprise will be revealed for all to see. In other words, technology is a way of life which can only continue all the time that no questions whatsoever are raised over its status and credibility. Yet the activity of the reflexive intellectuals meant nothing other than the raising of such questions.

For the reflexive intellectuals, the dominance of technology was something which was crying out for deconstruction. As Robert Musil put it of mathematics in the first volume of *The Man Without Qualities*, 'all those who have to know something about the soul . . . bear witness to the fact that it has been ruined by mathematics'. For these witness-bearers, according to Musil's not terribly flattering portrayal (after all, to a large extent he is talking of our ancestors, dear reader), 'in mathematics is the source of a wicked intellect that, while making man the lord of the earth, also makes him the slave of the machine' (Musil 1953: 40). This sentence can be used as a very fine summary of the thesis of the 'Dialectic of Enlightenment'. For them (for us?), 'mathematics, the mother of the exact sciences, the grandmother of engineering, was also the arch-mother of that spirit from which, in the end, poison-gases and fighter aircraft have been born' (Musil 1953: 41).

Musil helps develop an appreciation of the tendency of the reflexive intellectuals to deconstruct to their own satisfaction at least the narrative association of technology with improvement and civilization (the move exemplified by Martin Heidegger), whilst leaving technology itself largely untouched. This is one of the points which Musil tried to make; whilst a technical knowledge like science could be criticized, it was precisely the criticism which led to a recommitment on the part of mathematicians to their work: 'As far as Ulrich was concerned . . . it could at least definitely be said that he loved mathematics because of the people who could not endure it' (Musil 1953: 41). (Ulrich is the eponymous 'Man Without Qualities'.)

Perhaps something like the view from the vantage point of the carers of the soul can be found in the work of Max Weber. For Weber, the pretensions of any and all claims to the rational life stood in need of deconstruction on compelling moral grounds at least. But typically, Weber missed the point that to reveal the emptiness of rational activities is actually to do very little to the activities themselves. Anything can be said, but nothing changes. Yet Weber arguably went further than most others in uncovering the abyss of meaning which the modern institutions and arrangements glossed over. Weber realized that 'The various great ways of leading a rational and methodical life have been characterized by irrational presuppositions, which have been accepted simply as "given" and which have been incorporated into such ways of life' (Weber 1948: 281). Or, to give this insight some detail, according to Max Weber (and arguably he is here simply saying something which the other reflexive intellectuals were struggling to grasp for themselves), technology is its own legitimation; it serves no end other than that which it can give itself, no end other than its own propagation. But even though its ultimate vacuity is clear to those who care to look, still this form of the 'rational and methodical life' goes on.

The modern relationships and activities imply a situation in which the post-modern condition confronts but does not contain a technology which continues of its own accord, seemingly obeying nothing other than its own logic of development. Certainly, it remains possible to argue that technology is still the set of material activities by and through which the order of things is defended and established, and certainly it remains possible to suggest that technology is something like the motor of the linear history of the societal. But the profound difficulty which confronts the post-modern is that the post-modern groups do not perceive themselves as being in the driving seat of this increasingly rapid journey to the future. Quite the contrary, they tend to perceive themselves as powerless passengers who are taken to a destination they do not know and probably will not like even if they arrive. That is, if any destination can be imagined. In other words, it seems to be reasonable to suggest that at least in so far as the problems surrounding technology are concerned, the post-modern condition is in some ways like the 'risk society' described by Ulrich Beck.

With the notion of the risk society, Beck is trying to suggest that there is something unique about contemporary social and cultural conditions. According to Beck's very interesting analysis, conventional modern industrial arrangements cannot be understood in terms of a risk society because, in those arrangements, there is a kind of security pact. The pact means that potential hazards in the future are insured against in the present. This contract between future and present is expressed in the narrative of progress. As Beck writes, in modern industrial arrangements, 'a norm system of rules for social accountability, compensation and precautions, always very controversial in its details, creates present security in the face of an open uncertain future' (Beck 1992: 100). However, in the risk society (Beck does not talk about post-modernity or the post-modern), the situation is different. In the risk society the contract between future and present has been torn up. Instead of a technologically guaranteed progress the risk society is typified by a sense of the independence of technology.

In particular, and perhaps perfectly reasonably, Ulrich Beck is haunted by the possibilities of nuclear technology. He argues that 'nuclear power plants have suspended the principle of insurance not only in the economic, but also in the medical, psychological, cultural and religious sense. *The residual risk society has become an uninsured society*' (Beck 1992: 101). Instead of progress and the future, the inhabitants of the risk society know only short-term calculations of danger. The calculations are predicated upon technology. In no way do they question technology. 'In this sense, one could say that the calculus of risk exemplifies a type of ethics without morality, the mathematical ethics of the technological age' (Beck 1992: 99). A morality which goes nowhere other than to the next scenario of possible risk and fear.

However, and against Beck's own position, it seems to be quite reasonable to suggest that it is only from within the spaces of the post-modern condition that technology can be perceived as an aspect and agent of something called the risk society. The risk society is itself a single dimension of the condition of post-modernity. This is because it is only in a post-modern condition that two situations are held to prevail. Firstly, the ostensible ends of technology have been deconstructed so that technology is an end in itself. As Ulrich Beck says, 'the place of the "categorical imperative" is taken by the mortality rates under certain conditions of air pollution' (Beck 1992: 99). Secondly, the narratives of linear time have been transcended so that it is largely impossible to steer technology in a single and universally legitimate direction.

Now, if these aspects of the post-modern condition are brought together, a highly fractured and problematic picture emerges. Part of the problem is due to the nature of the post-modern social and cultural groups. The inhabitants of the post-modern are rather like nomads. They are tied to a single time and place. They cannot really be characterized by a single fixed identity and neither therefore, can it be said that they follow a single and exclusive path of history. In many ways, that is precisely what it means to be an intellectual who has managed to deconstruct the narratives which historically justified technology (in another way, it is also what it means to be an intellectual who practises reflexivity after the Party). It is also what it means to participate in the social and cultural groups which coalesce around surface performances.

The intellectuals and the performers are certainly very different but they are also very similar. They have discovered the secret that there are no secrets. As such, they are not involved in the relationships of the production of either hermeneutic or material goods. Primarily they practise so many activities of consumption (the things consumed can either be intellectual through the deconstruction of the taken for granted, or material through the use of styles and goods which others have already made). They operate on stages which have already been constituted.

However, technology continues to exist. It has no socially imposed purpose. Indeed, only the most modern of the technicians claims to have any hold whatsoever over the steering wheel (but in the eyes of the post-modern groups, such members of the modern technical intelligentsia have lost legitimacy in any case). Technology still propels social and cultural relationships along the path of a linear time which post-modernity has long since abandoned. Consequently, from the point of view of the post-modern social and cultural groups, technology and, more broadly the world itself, tends to be interpreted as something which is out of control. For them, the socially and societally produced nature is now tending to be defining of what it means to live in this world. It would appear that nature is taking its revenge on the claims of social and societal reflexivity.

The post-modern condition is then, riddled with a deep and probably irreconcilable cleavage between social and cultural tendencies on one side and material tendencies on the other. Whereas for modernity those two tendencies were, in principle at least, moving in much the same direction at much the same pace, for post-modernity they are pulling apart from each other. This raises the most serious ethical questions.

One of the most profound reflections on the ethical implications of technology has been offered by Hans Jonas. Although he does not deal with categories like modernity and post-modernity, his arguments are compelling and extremely helpful for an understanding of the stakes and the terrain of post-modernity. Basically, Jonas' point is that technology makes demands and has implications which the orthodox ethical resources of social and societal reciprocity and responsibility are quite unable to meet. Jonas says that the processes of technology can be defined in terms of the expansion of the 'artificial environment' (Jonas 1984: 9). Yet he comments that 'Modern technology has introduced actions of such novel scale, objects, and consequences that the framework of former ethics can no longer contain them' (Jonas 1984: 6).

According to Jonas, traditional ethics are predicated on the assumption of a double immediacy. These codes assume that the future which is relevant to the actions of the subject stretches no further than an individual life. They also assume that ethically relevant actions involve largely face to face interaction. As Jonas puts it, these ethical systems presuppose that 'The ethical universe is composed of contemporaries, and its horizon to the future is confined by the foreseeable span of their lives' (Jonas 1984: 5). Or, put another way, I have no responsibility for the world after my death. This assumption of immediacy was symbolized by the city which represented a bounded universe of human self-definition. According to Jonas, since the time of the ancient Greeks, the city has been interpreted as a haven of reflexivity in a universe of otherwise natural reification: 'It is in this intrahuman frame ... that all traditional ethics dwells, and it matches the size of action delimited by this frame' (Jonas 1984: 4). The boundary walls of the city indicated the limits of the milieu of societal self-construction: 'this citadel of his own making, clearly set off from the rest of things and entrusted to him, was the whole and sole domain of man's responsible action'. Jonas continues to spell out the implications of this bounded milieu for the relationship with the world which was identified as without bounds: 'Nature was not an object of human responsibility – she taking care of herself and, with some coaxing and worrying, also of man: not ethics, only cleverness applied to her' (Jonas 1984: 4).

But the development and employment of technological resources, and of course, the construction of the bounded milieu of ethical responsibility (that is, the construction of the city), means that the previously direct matching of the moral with the societal universe has been disrupted. The technological resources which once built the city walls high and mighty have now demolished them. According to Hans Jonas, technology means that we now have to deal with the world which we previously saw as nothing more than a standing-reserve waiting for animation by us. 'The containment of nearness and contemporaneity is gone, swept away by the spatial spread and time span of the cause-effect trains which technological practice sets afoot, even when undertaken for proximate ends' (Jonas 1984: 7). As such, 'the boundary between "city" and "nature" has been obliterated: the city of men, once an enclave in the nonhuman world, spreads over the whole of terrestrial nature and usurps its place' (Jonas 1984: 10). Thanks to the ability of technology to quite transcend the immediacy and bounded contexts of time and place there has emerged 'a growing realm of collective action where doer, deed, and effect are no longer the same as they were in the proximate sphere' (Jonas 1984: 6).

Furthermore, Jonas suggests that the increasing abilities of technology mean that Man has become an object, instead of the subject, of technological activity and ordering. For example, through technology it is now possible to extend the life span of the individual. Whereas previous ethics dealt with the problem of how to come to terms with the unalterable fact of death, the ethics for the technological age also has to come to terms with the possibility that physical life can be extended. This raises a number of questions. On the relatively mundane level, there is now the need to confront practical dilemmas of whose life will be extended? how will the extension be paid for? who will decide? But there are also serious metaphysical difficulties which 'involve the very meaning of our finitude, the attitude toward death, and the general biological significance of the balance of death and procreation' (Jonas 1984: 18). Jonas also points to the problems and possibilities of genetic engineering and argues that they 'show most vividly how far our powers to act are pushing us beyond the terms of all former ethics' (Jonas 1984: 21).

Jonas expresses grave concerns about the situation which might prevail if it does not prove possible to develop the ethical resources which are demanded and forced by technology. He suggests, perhaps unsurprisingly, that if ethics cannot take hold of technological possibilities, then technology will continue regardless and become increasingly defining of what it means and is to be human. In other words, Jonas is saying that even forgetting about the possibility of ecological disaster, technology promises the moral and existential disaster of the reification of humanity. Here then, it is possible to identify another rendition of the theme most brilliantly expressed by Marx that increasing material ability and richness goes hand in hand with decreasing humanity. Jonas confronts the current situation with a withering gaze. He says that at the moment, when technology has indeed reduced the human to an object of manipulation but before the ethical resources required to meet the challenge of technology have been developed, humanity stands cold, trembling and alone: 'Now we shiver in the nakedness of a nihilism in which near-omnipotence is paired with near-emptiness, greatest capacity with knowing least for what ends to use it' (Jonas 1984: 23).

But Jonas enjoins that we simply must learn how to use our powers; we simply must define the meaning of technology for ourselves and thus rescue the human and for that matter the natural from a moral and material devastation. Jonas forces a recognition that what might be called the contemporary human condition should be one of a resolute and honest confrontation with the impact and effects of our technological productions. Jonas wants us to acknowledge, and act on the basis of, our responsibility for unforeseeable effects of which we are the causes. That responsibility cannot be qualified or passed over to narratives of History or Reason. Neither of course are the conventional ethical resources available to us (after all, it is precisely the inability of the traditional resources to come to terms with technology which stimulates the transcendence of the city of ends in the first place). For Jonas, we are on our own; we must come to terms with our moral and material condition in what he calls the 'technological age'. Consequently, he presses an ethic of responsibility.

For Hans Jonas, it is imperative (in both the ethical and the urgent senses of the word) that we construct and obey an ethic of responsibility which upholds a duty to care for the 'future of mankind'. But the concentration on 'mankind' does not mean that we care for other humans alone. Jonas' point is that any care for the future of humanity necessarily also means a care for the future of nature. Quite simply, humanity has no future if the planet has no future. Therefore, any care for the future of mankind logically requires a care for the future of the earth. Jonas is arguing that with this ethic of responsibility we need not demolish all technology out of hand. Rather, his point is that we should always attend to the overwhelmingly destructive potential of technology. Consequently, Jonas sees the care for the future as something like a 'metaphysical responsibility beyond self-interest'. This responsibility 'has devolved on us with the magnitude of our powers relative to this tenuous film of life, that is, since man has become dangerous not only to himself but to the whole biosphere' (Jonas 1984: 136). Simply put then, Jonas' ethic is one which preaches and embodies caution. He upholds: 'in a time of one-sided pressures and mounting risks ... the side of moderation and circumspection, of "beware!" and "preserve!" ' (Jonas 1984: 204).

Now, Hans Jonas has undoubtedly developed an analysis of the moral and material implications of technology which must be taken seriously. He makes serious points and proposes serious, but far from easy or reassuring answers. It might even be said that in terms of ethical speculation and theory construction at least, Hans Jonas goes a very long way towards resolving the difficulties with which technology confronts post-modernity. Jonas' ethic of responsibility does seem to be persuasive. But sociologically, there is a major problem with all of this. Perhaps even the unquiet slumbers which Hans Jonas promises are rather too much to expect. Basically, whilst the ethic of responsibility which Jonas enjoins is both pertinent and necessary, there seem to be few if any reasons to imagine that the social and cultural groups which occupy the condition of post-modernity are possessed of the existential and hermeneutic resources which will enable them to develop that ethic. Even less are they likely to be able to live up to the demands made by Hans Jonas.

Jonas writes that 'technological power has turned what used and ought to be tentative, perhaps enlightening plays of speculative reason into competing blueprints for projects, and in choosing between them we have to choose between extremes of remote effects' (Jonas 1984: 21). Arguably, Jonas is making a perfectly valid and correct point. The problem is that he assumes an ability to choose. But if attention is being directed to the conditions of existence of the post-modern, that might well be a rather wild assumption to make.

Jonas wants attention to the future. But that attention presupposes that the future stands in some direct linear relation to the present and indeed, that technology itself can be brought back under social control if enough energy is expended. However, the post-modern condition intimates precisely the opposite.

Firstly, narratives of a single linearity linking past, present and future through the fixed identity of pilgrim-like groups such as the proletariat or narratives such as progress and civilization are incoherent. The incoherence is simply attributable to the logical absurdity of pilgrimage-like activities and identities. Secondly, although the walls of the city of ends might well have been demolished, this does not mean that humanity is able to wander freely from place to place. Quite the contrary. Confronted with the virtually absolute freedom which lies on the other side of the boundaries of modernity, the social groups which wander outside rather tend to lose all their bearings and indeed, the ability to find new ones. After all, this is the essence of their nomad-like condition of existence. Thirdly, of course, technology is perceived as something outside of the hermeneutic and existential conditions which are typical of post-modernity. It is not interpreted as something which is open to attempts at gaining control. It is instead understood as something rather more by way of a second nature. It goes its own way whilst social and cultural activities go theirs. In a nutshell, the future does not belong to the post-modern social and cultural groups. They do not know what it is, they do not know what it means and therefore, they lack the hermeneutic and existential resources to be able to be responsible for it. As T.S. Eliot rightly said in *Little Gidding*, 'A people without history is not redeemed from time' (Eliot 1982).

Indeed, it is this irredeemability from history which is perhaps, the most significant aspect of what I have been calling the nomad-like nature of the post-modern groups. A sense of history was a fundamental dimension of the modern identities. Time would redeem the identities of suffering or want in the present and thus, the passage of history was interpreted also as the passage towards the moment of arrival. This is why I have been calling the modern identities *pilgrim-like*. However, to the extent that the post-modern condition in many ways revolves around the impossibility of arrival, and indeed of the inappropriateness of any single trajectory of time, so its typical groups are never able to go anywhere. From the point of view of post-modernity, time and history redeem nothing simply because there is nothing to be redeemed (after all there are no longer the fixed identities of wanting) and, moreover, no condition of the redemption.

But perhaps the situation is more complex yet. The technology which secured an order of things in the modern and for that matter the post-modern world contains the distinct chance that there will be no future. Any conception of the future, even the conception that the future is absolutely unintelligible, is only possible if it is taken for granted that either the world will continue after the death of the individual or that the anthropological figure of Man will go on regardless of however many individual men might die. But some of the uses of technology which appeared in the twentieth century mean that neither guarantees of the future can be taken for granted anymore. Technology now implies the possibility, not just of the death of men but, also of the death of Man. Thanks to the possibility of the nuclear holocaust, it is possible that all individual humans could die at the same time and that therefore, the grand modern hero of Man will disappear as well. As Harry Redner has said, 'The present danger of the mortality of Man derives ultimately from the universal mortality of men. Men are mortal . . . therefore Man is mortal.' Redner continues in an understandably pessimistic vein: 'If one were to follow that line of reasoning to the bitter end one would have to conclude finally that not only Man is mortal but that Man will most certainly be dead, and that very likely soon' (Redner 1982: 20).

All the time that the continuation of Man could be simply assumed, the lives of individuals could be identified as yet another kind of pilgrimage. To live was to be like a pilgrim on the road to death. But that death would be meaningful and significant for those who continue to live (even though it is meaningless for the individual who dies; once again, transformation with arrival renders pilgrimage-like journeys quite absurd). It is meaningful simply because those who go on living remain to bear witness to the dead. Furthermore, each individual knows in principle that some others or something called Man will continue after his or her death (even Adorno struggled perhaps against the odds, to cling to this hope, despite his announcement of the moral death of Man in the material death of men at Auschwitz; Adorno 1973).

But the possibilities associated with nuclear technology in particular involve a radical and quite drastic transformation of this situation. This recognition is specifically post-modern because it represents a transcendence of the legitimating modern narratives of nuclear techno-logy. Those legitimations tie nuclear technology to destinies such as reproducible power or reproducible peace. And of course, they assert that any nuclear holocaust (of whatever origin; accidental or designed) is absolutely impossible. The reflection on the possibility of the death of Man thanks to nuclear technology is indeed an incredulity towards the metanarratives of the peaceful atom and deterrence.

The nuclear holocaust is just one especially awful instance of a far broader set of occurrences. The possibilities implied by this technology mean that death might well become meaningless and that therefore, the life of the individual will be no longer like a pilgrimage. This series of possibilities even surrounds more mundane daily activities. After all, 'Technological progress has made of dying a controllable physiological process in which the individual undergoing it is uninvolved; he is kept alive or allowed to go under at the behest of physicians and lawyers' (Redner 1982: 23). Or indeed, at the behest of the military. Redner says that the individual 'can no longer prepare himself for that last moment of truth and submit to it as a fatality beyond human intervention. His death is no longer his own – except, perhaps, when he deliberately chooses it in suicide' (Redner 1982: 23).

But if all men die at the moment of my suicide, and I do not know for sure that they will not (the chance of the nuclear holocaust has taken away that certainty for ever), it still lacks truth because it is possible that there will be nobody and no thing to bear witness to my suicide. This is all part of the 'new meaninglessness of death' (Redner 1982: 23). Death is meaningless because, through the effects of technology, it has been subjected to a kind of slicing away of the possibility of meaningfulness. Death has been reified as largely meaningless when, for Redner at least, death should be the site and occasion of great enterprises in reflexivity.

Death should be socially and culturally defined as important and significant, rather than technologically defined as empty and insignificant.

Indeed, this kind of belief means that despite the frequently pessimistic tone of the argument, Harry Redner does not give way to total despair. He knows that technology implies and intimates the reification of death. But he believes that an effort must be made to recall the deaths of the dead; to recall the circumstances and meanings of those deaths and thus, rescue them from a once and for all definition from which any escape is quite impossible. In other words, Redner wants us to remember death and consequently, construct and reconstruct its meanings for ourselves. After Auschwitz, poetry becomes less possible and more necessary. He advocates the practice of a reflexivity which also involves an expansion of the qualities and capacities of what it is to be human. Redner sees 'the recollective task of finding a voice for all these modes of dying. This is the ultimate form of the Orphic quest: by means of the voice to recover death from oblivion' (Redner 1982: 288–9). Out of a reflection and remembering of death, through the reinsertion of death into the everyday, Redner believes it is possible to replenish the resources of social and cultural reflexivity: 'To be cut off completely from the dead would constitute another kind of death for which we as yet have no name . . . a total amnesia of the human race' (Redner 1982: 288). Technology threatens precisely that amnesia.

Without that rediscovery and recollection of the essential humanity of death (rather than a dwelling on the threat of the death of humanity), the post-modern condition of a kind of nomadism is given another twist. Here, it would be made metaphysical. Without reflexivity, the technological death is simply a reinforcement of the nomad-like condition of existence. Life, of the individual as of the figure of Man, cannot really be interpreted as like some kind of pilgrimage towards whatever and wherever. Instead, without the social definition of its meaning, death becomes a dull and frightening fact (once again, it becomes an event which simply happens with all the force of a natural compulsion). Or it is simply taken to be a demonstration of one more thing which technology will make passive one day.

But arguably, those efforts and exploits of reflexivity remain to be accomplished. And indeed, just as there seems to be no convincing sociological reason to believe that the ethic of responsibility which Hans Jonas enjoins is actually capable of production in the condition of post-modernity, so it seems hard to find a persuasive reason to imagine where the resources will come from which will inspire the post-modern groups to think the meanings of their potential deaths. After all, and as Immanuel Kant recognized at the very threshold of modernity, 'it is so much easier and so much more comforting to believe what others say; it is so much easier not to think for oneself' (Kant 1970). It is certainly much more pleasant not to have to confront the moral implications of the fact of one's own material death.

The post-modern condition intimates a series of relationships and processes in which both life and death are reified into a simple repetition, a simple cycle of sociality until the apocalyptic moment of the death of all men and of Man. Life and death can only be a pointless and circular occurrence because there is no universal home or purpose of Man which is the destination of the journey to death. Consequently there is, in this metaphysical sense, no purpose to life and death. Both are actually quite pointless outside of the entirely temporary meanings which can be created in the here and now. But since those meanings are trapped in the present, they cannot be fixed and rendered permanent over time. They imply nothing other than their own lack of permanence and essential compulsion.

Indeed, the endless repetition and lack of any linear movement is practised more and more frantically and more and more enthusiastically, precisely so that the implications of the lack of a meaningful end need never be faced. However, this does not mean that the post-modern condition is one of a complete hedonism and of a complete lack of responsibility. Quite the contrary, it is the question of responsibility which haunts all of the activities of the post-modern groups. But that responsibility is not to grand narratives like the future of humanity or the future of the planet. Rather, it is more by way of a responsibility to avoid the abyss of meaning by disguising in a flurry of activity or a socially induced metaphysical cretinism the utter pointlessness of social and cultural activity.

In other words, the material and traditionally the moral fact of mortality is pushed aside. Instead, the post-modern condition operates in terms of an assumption of what might be called the wager on the immortality of the present. Since the post-modern is trapped in the present, so it is logically immortal as well. This immortality can be explained as a product of two factors. Firstly it is by no means self-evident that anyone or anything will continue after the individual death to bear witness to that mortality. Secondly the post-modern does not occupy a moment on a trajectory of historical time. Rather it is here and now for ever.

Unsurprisingly, the situation has profound sociological and moral implications. Perhaps they have been captured best by Jorge Luis Borges, another writer of literature who, like Franz Kafka, Robert Musil and a number of others says rather more things of sociological significance than most sociologists. Of course, the argument becomes extremely metaphorical, but Borges writes that for mortals and for the inhabitants of the condition of mortality, 'every act they execute may be their last; there is not a face that is not on the verge of dissolving like a face in a dream' (Borges 1970: 146). This is a situation of once and never again. It might also be seen as approaching an intimation of modernity with its relentless quest for the future. But in the condition of immortality, within the boundless terrain without the intimation of mortality, the situation is radically different. There, according to Borges, 'every act (and every thought) is the echo of others that preceded it in the past, with no visible beginning, or the faithful presage of others that in the future will repeat it to a vertiginous degree' (Borges 1970: 146). Arguably this passage with its picture of an endless circularity and lack of destination can be read as a most accurate summary of the sociological characteristics and activities of the post-modern condition.

Basically then the central problem which runs through the relationships and categories of post-modernity is the question of responsibility. Thanks to technology, the inhabitants of post-modernity should be responsible in a way which was previously unimaginable. They should be responsible not just for their immediate actions and effects in the bounded universe of the city of ends. They should be also responsible for the very possibility of the future of Man and Nature alike. To this extent, technology means that humanity must indeed roam throughout the universe either leaving new cautionary tracks to keep out trespassers or desperately trying to erase the asphalt motorways of the not so long gone ancestors. But the reifying impact and implication of technology seems to intimate the tragedy that the social and cultural resources which typify the post-modern condition are actually not adequate to nourish the ethic of responsibility. Quite simply, technology and particularly the practical lesson of some of the ways technology might be used, implies that there might actually be no future beyond my own death. As such, it is impossible to develop an ethic of responsibility because it is by no means clear what the post-modern groups should be responsible for. The future as such? Or the possibility of a future?

To this extent, then, technology radically restricts the possibilities and potentials of existence. Technology destroys the chances of the responsibility which is so desperately needed to keep technology in check and under the sway of social and cultural definition. This is the essential paradox of the post-modern dialectic of technology; responsibility for the future without the inevitability of a future. But, as a kind of unwanted prize, that paradox gives post-modernity the Holy Grail of a great deal of previous social and cultural activity. The key to the possibility of immortality.

Chapter 6

Others

In many ways, it might be said that the curious and boring possibility of immortality which is to some extent implied by an analysis of the post-modern condition is something like a very mundane metaphysical wager. After all, and as Borges said, 'To be immortal is commonplace; except for man, all creatures are immortal, for they are ignorant of death'. But Borges continues with a warning: 'what is divine, terrible, incomprehensible, is to know that one is immortal' (Borges 1970: 144). In these terms, post-modernity suggests the chance that we (the 'we' that is, constituted by those who live the life of post-modernity) and all others have become ignorant of our deaths and of death itself as a universal social and cultural condition. Death is surrounded with ignorance to a much greater extent than ever before simply because now, the continuation of something universal after the moment of individual death cannot be taken for granted. Technology has helped make sure of that.

But post-modernity also involves the daily attempt to deny this rather abstract intimation of immortality. After all, to always live in the face of immortality, however mundane and terrible it might be, is to make life itself quite incomprehensible. If it is reasonable to propose that the modern relationships played no small part in hiding the problem of mortality, so it is also the case that the post-modern relationships play a part in hiding the problem of immortality.

As a metaphorical illustration of this point, it is worth looking at Borges' story once again. The immortals of Borges' story failed to overcome the knowledge of immortality. They did not participate in the kind of ceaseless social and cultural activity which would have left no time for contemplation on the end of all things. They had achieved immortality through the creation of beautiful cultural artifacts like the *Odyssey*. But unfortunately these immortals had rested on their laurels. Borges' immortals lived by the assumption that it is enough to create beauty once. For them a single act of creation was supposed to overcome mortality. Perhaps they had been right; perhaps their cultural production did indeed mean that they never died (the individual called Homer might well disappear but the name and the symbol, the reflexivity, of Homer continues for all time). But the immortals had quite missed the point that immortality too can never be confronted. Borges' immortals are divine and yet terrible precisely because they cannot hide their self-produced immortality from themselves.

Of course, it is not the case that the social and cultural groups of post-modernity actually are immortal in any physical sense. To pretend that they are would be just a little ridiculous. As individuals they must die and become ill exactly like everyone else (although whether the individuals who suffer a long death are able to retain their post-modernity is rather another matter; this point will be developed later). That is, after all, the lot of all biological organisms (even though some people try to avoid the finality of death through deep freezing and other forms of technological intervention. But these techniques do not free the individual from reification. Instead, they merely place her or him in other relationships of dependency. The technology lives.).

Neither does the possibility of immortality necessarily mean that the post-modern condition involves a resurgence of religious or spiritual concerns. It does not necessarily suggest a re-enchantment of the world in relation to the modern situation which was so often taken to be synonymous with the disenchantment of the world (an argument which has been a commonplace of sociology since Weber at least). The post-modern hint of immortality is actually far more trivial than that. But perhaps it is also therefore rather more of a burden to have to bear.

The problem is that this kind of immortality has serious implications for the hermeneutic and existential concern to make the present make sense. If it is not unreasonable to place a bet on the chance that nothing will survive me, then my life in the here and now is denied any ultimate goal (because it is quite possible that it will be impossible for my achievement of that goal to be known, and thus impossible for my life to be judged a success or failure). Moreover any sense of the continuity of a linear time called history becomes rather less than entirely self-evident. The implications and consequences of technology (its consequences for the societal, the social and the natural) make any kind of confidently forward looking philosophical or sociological assumptions seem quite untenable. As such, this particular kind of intimation of immortality reduces the metaphysical to the physical (if indeed, it does not actually mean the reduction of the metaphysical to little more than an empty husk for cheap consolation or crass pieces of profundity in pop songs).

The post-modern intimates a kind of immortality because it is a condition which is lived and formed (I use those words in a Simmelian sense) in the shadow of the possibility of apocalypse. And indeed, the very status of the apocalypse as something which might or might not happen, which might only be known after it has started and when therefore, any response is already too late, makes its threats even worse than they might be otherwise. However likely the apocalypse might be, it is impossible to know for sure whether or not it will actually occur or whether indeed, it is occurring already. (Has the ecological apocalypse begun? It is virtually impossible to say.)

The threat of apocalypse consequently has a double effect. Firstly, it implies the redundancy of any narratives which are projected into the future or which simply take for granted a more or less infinite continuation of Man. Secondly, it reinforces and adds another dimension to what can be called the nomad-like aspects of the post-modern condition. The chance that everything will explode means that there is no direction, no ultimate purpose to activity in the here and now. But that activity must take place relentlessly and with desperate enthusiasm. Its futility from a teleological point of view can never be generally accepted, or else only ennui and anomie will result. If anything, the futility requires enthusiasm.

All there can be is a creation of meaning in the present. There can be no fixed identities and no fixed meanings. Neither can there be fixed values. Once again, this situation was unerringly illustrated in the story written by Borges. He speculated that 'Because of his past or future virtues, every man is worthy of all goodness, but also of all perversity, because of his infamy in the past or future'. Borges continues to note that 'Seen in this manner, all our acts are just, but they are also indifferent. There are no moral or intellectual merits' (Borges 1970: 145). (Compare with the condition of emotivism which is seen as prevalent by Alastair MacIntyre: see MacIntyre 1985.)

Some of the implications of the imagination of the chance of the apocalypse have been explored in an interesting way by Susan Sontag. She observes that conceptions of linear time 'need the confirmation of their images, so our reaction to events in the present seeks confirmation in a mental outline, with appropriate computations, of the event in its projected, ultimate form' (Sontag 1991: 174). For example, in the linear time assumed by the Marxist narrative, the oppression of the proletariat in the present is confirmed by the imagination of the revolution in the future. But Sontag's point is that it is possible to call forth not just utopian but also dystopian imaginations of the future. But of course the representations of terrible futures call into doubt the very status of linear time itself. Sontag suggests that 'the look into the future, which was once tied to a vision of linear progress, has, with more knowledge at our disposal than anyone could have dreamed, turned into a vision of disaster' (Sontag 1991: 175).

Consequently, according to Sontag, the future is collapsed into the present and the present becomes something which is largely incomprehensible: 'There is what is happening now. And there is what it portends: the imminent, but not yet actual, and really graspable, disaster' (Sontag 1991: 175). Or, put another way, the future ceases to be a future. The inhabitants of post-modernity are required now to uphold a responsibility for the future and yet they (we) lack the resources for that obligation.

Indeed, Susan Sontag also realizes that the apocalyptic imaginations tend to result in a hermeneutic and existential denial of the apocalypse itself. The denial takes either of two connected forms.

Firstly, according to Sontag, 'A proliferation of reports or projections of unreal (that is, ungraspable) doomsday eventualities tends to produce a variety of reality-denying responses' (Sontag 1991: 176). The greater the announced likelihood of apocalypse, the more it is practically denied. The apocalypse ceases to be the single event of the destruction of everything simply because, thanks to all the reports, the apocalypse seems to be coming from so many different directions at the same time. The apocalypse fractures into lots of little apocalypses (but virtually by definition there cannot be more than one apocalypse). By way of a development of this insight, Sontag suggests that the more we worry about the moment of the apocalypse, the more it is necessary to forget the fears generated in the present. For example, Susan Sontag points out that the rational justifications for nuclear weapons only hold good if the reality of individual fears of the nuclear holocaust are ignored. The reality of living in the shadow of the possibility of the nuclear apocalypse is denied a reality. Similarly, a number of national governments deny the reality of the warnings which are made about global warming even though the warnings are often made by the scientists who are believed when they say that global warming is not taking place (although of course, this kind of denial contains a considerable amount of political expediency).

Secondly, the chance of the apocalypse is denied through a strategy of banalization so that the seamlessness of dystopia comes to seem inevitable. The apocalypse becomes a simple fact of life. Turning to the question of AIDS, Sontag writes that 'the fear of AIDS is of a piece with attention to other unfolding disasters that are by-products of advanced society, particularly those illustrating the degradation of the environment on a world scale'. She continues: 'AIDS is one of the dystopian harbingers of the global village, that future which is already here and before us, which no one knows how to refuse' (Sontag 1991: 178). The imagination of the death of the inhabitants of the global village through the spread of AIDS is simply one of the mundane and boring facts of living in this world. It is a future which is already here. It plays no small part in defining the life of post-modernity.

The collapse of the horizons of linear time goes hand in hand with the collapse of the narratives which give a goal, a direction and indeed a seemingly intrinsic or inevitable purpose to social and cultural activity. The imagination of the unimaginable and absolute boundary of the apocalypse actually intimates a condition of boundlessness. Consequently, it implies a perpetual and ever-present confrontation with contingency. Whereas the identification of historical goals implies also the identification of certain kinds of necessity (such as the necessity of the class struggle, or the necessity of the moral regulation of the otherwise anomic individual, or whatever), so the transcendence of the goals means also the transcendence of necessity. Instead, there is only contingency.

To put the matter somewhat schematically, it can be proposed that if modernity involves a burying of contingency through the reification of forms, then post-modernity involves an emergence of contingency through the transcendence of forms. However, the struggle of life in post-modernity implies a refusal to face up to this contingent boundlessness.

An early hint of this problem and dialectic of contingency can be found in Joris-Karl Huysmans' short novel, *Downstream* (Huysmans 1952). On the face of it, the story told by Huysmans is at once deeply melancholy and fairly tedious. It tells of the futile search of Jean Folantin, a poorly paid clerk in nineteenth century Paris, to find a good meal. The novel is about the trials and tribulations of this endless and never fulfilled search. Folantin tries every kind of restaurant in every part of Paris and yet his quest for a slice of meat which is edible and for a piece of cheese which is not rancid is never successful. On this superficial level, Huysmans' story is not very interesting. But the point is that the quest of Jean Folantin is intended to be read as a metaphor of a quest for a kind of existential contentment in the urban landscape of commodified exchange (the very strong connection between the city and commodified exchange was, of course, demonstrated by Georg Simmel; see Simmel 1990. For a very stimulating exploration of the specific Parisian situation which is the background for Huysmans, see Clark 1985).

Indeed, the Paris which is the landscape for *Downstream* is also the

Paris of Baudelaire's *Feuilleton*. It is a landscape of the modern building of the bounded universe of the societal. It is a landscape in which everything which time and memory had established as the natural has either been turned into an ornament or into something to be uprooted tomorrow. Within this wholly fabricated milieu, the chance of aesthetic and existential nourishment is sensed as having disappeared. It has been replaced by the fleeting and rapid relationships of the exchange of commodities.

Once, Folantin had been a Baudelairian *flâneur* who constituted the life of the urban in his own subjective gaze. But subsequently he was trapped by the forms of the metropolis. Its architecture and morality determined and defined his life for him. Once, in the nostalgically recalled 'old days' (a nostalgia which simultaneously condemns the present and yet makes existence in it that little bit easier), Folantin had been 'happy to saunter along the forgotten alleys and the poor, provincial-looking streets, catching a glimpse through ground-floor windows of the private lives of the people who lived there' (Huysmans 1952: 31). But now the urban landscape is a place of fear and trembling. All of the old dwellings of life have been replaced by forms which define and discipline what happen within them. 'Everything had vanished: no more clumps of foliage, no more trees – instead, unending barracks stretching as far as the eye could see.' Huysmans continues: 'In this new Paris, M. Folantin felt faint and sick at heart.' Not least, Jean Folantin's existential sickness was because 'he was the sort who loathed the new type of shop' (Huysmans 1952: 31).

Basically, Huysmans is not making the trivial claim that it is hard to find a good meal in the city. Rather he is saying that modernity makes the quest for satisfaction impossible to accomplish. But Huysmans also realizes that despite its intrinsic futility in the world of 'endless barracks' and gas-lit shops, the quest for satisfaction can never be given up. Reflecting on his failure, 'M. Folantin began to wonder if it were worthwhile chopping and changing . . . But he decided to persevere – "If I keep on looking, I might find something," he said – and went on combing the eating-houses and small restaurants' (Huysmans 1952: 16). To this extent then, *Downstream* can be interpreted fairly readily as an especially clear modern tale of the pilgrimage-like activities of the attempts to find the truth of the order of things. Folantin is always searching for something which he is confident he will find tomorrow (the melancholic despair of Huysmans' story being due to the half-intuited realization that tomorrow will never come).

Folantin is indeed more than a little like Emma Bovary. For both of them, the possibilities and options of life have been completely trapped by the reified forms. In the case of Emma Bovary the forms involve the restrictions and expectations of the stifling convention of the provincial bourgeoisie. In the case of Jean Folantin, they involve the disciplined and disciplining architecture of the Paris of Haussmann. All that is left for both of them is a kind of completely interiorized, psychological and (for Folantin) spiritual quest for compensation. But the problem is that the modern forms have taken such a hold that for both Bovary and Folantin the pilgrimage is largely unsuccessful (or at least it does not succeed in any way which can be reproduced).

At this level then, it cannot be doubted that *Downstream* is a tale of modern existence and modern identity. It is a classic modern tale of searching and not finding. But perhaps the charge of the story, and the reason why it is still worth reflecting on such a barren little tale, is due to the way it deals with the intimation of contingency. Admittedly, the intimation is never expressed clearly but it is possible to read *Downstream* as a story which pushes to the extreme limits of the reified and defining modern forms. But Joris-Karl Huysmans was a subject of the modern. As such, he desperately turns away from the glimpse of the contingency which lies without the bounds of modernity. Huysmans is typically modern in that as soon as he glimpses it, he struggles to bury contingency under the weight of social and cultural activities. Huysmans cannot, or at least does not, accept the possibility that things do not have to be like this.

Although Folantin is committed to the pilgrimage for a good meal, the dinner could actually be found anywhere in Paris. There is no single route to satisfaction and to the consummation of desire. There is no definite time and place in the future when it will be possible to drink a glass of adequate wine. In other words Huysmans uncovers the possibility that within the Paris of Folantin, there is no linear time. Neither might there be a resting place for the groups and individuals who search so hard for happiness. There is no one place of arrival. The spaces and the practices of Huysmans' character are therefore, to some extent intimated as more or less completely and yet disastrously contingent. Folantin might find a good meal, then again he might not. He might find it on the Right Bank, then again he might find it on the Left Bank. There is nothing definite, no guarantee.

But Huysmans' text demonstrates its modernity when it proves to be incapable of identifying or understanding that glimpse of the lack of necessity as in any way creative or constitutive. Huysmans simply cannot imagine contingency in any beneficial or constructive way. Instead, and since he has cut off the escape route of the possibility of the lack of necessity, all Huysmans can identify is a complete entrapment of the individual by the modern forms. The entrapment is itself the terrible response to the terrifying possibility of the abyss of meaning. For Huysmans, the city might be awful, but at least it is definitely awful.

The only response to the defining metropolis which Huysmans can imagine is one which largely accepts modernity at face value. His response is one of despair: 'As he made his way homewards, he saw life to be grim and desolate; he saw the futility of any change of course, any impulse, any effort; he saw that there was nothing to do but just drift downstream' (Huysmans 1952: 44). Huysmans' hero ceases to practice any history in and for himself. Instead, all he can do is hope that history will lead him to a good restaurant for reasons of its own, in the fullness of its own time. But at least that acceptance of definition by history means that contingency is avoided. The price of the denial of contingency is the impossibility of the individual and personal construction of linear time. For the individual who can do nothing other than go downstream, time seems to become a simple and endless looping back on itself. The past, the present and the future become identical if not quite inseparable. For the individual who is trapped in forms, there is actually no movement. After all, it is only history which goes downstream. At the end, Folantin remarks, 'I suppose the simplest thing to do is to go back to the old chop-house, and back tomorrow to the Ministerial sheep-pen' (Huysmans 1952: 44).

The post-modern condition emerges most fully as and when the reified forms of the edifices either collapse or are pushed over (but they are more likely to collapse of their own accord and because of their own structural weaknesses; an individual like Jean Folantin could hardly muster the energy and effort to do any pushing for himself. The only groups which do any important pushing for themselves are the reflexive intellectuals). With the collapse and transcendence, contingency emerges. Although Agnes Heller and Ferenc Fehér go so far as to imply that contingency is tantamount to the human condition on the neo-Heideggerian grounds that 'Each and every person is thrown into a particular world by the accident of birth' (Heller and Fehér 1988:15), they are nevertheless aware of the variability of the cultural attempts to come to terms with that contingency. In other words, they might well argue that Huysmans' character Folantin was thrown into a Paris which was objectively found rather than subjectively made. But Heller and Fehér would also suggest that his attempts to overcome the fact of contingency were peculiar to the circumstances of the modern European city (or even more specifically, of a modern European city).

According to Heller and Fehér, an initial contingency is typical of being in the world. After all, 'Nothing in our biological constitution or genetic endowments pre-determine that we should be born into one particular age than another, into one particular society rather than another, or into one particular social stratum rather than another' (Heller and Fehér 1988: 15–16). The point is however, that invariably any social and societal existence is only taken to be sustainable if the location of any individual is identified as in some way necessary. Heller and Fehér propose that 'Denizens of the premodern world mobilized vast ideological resources to shield the social arrangements of domination and hierarchy against the awareness of contingency.' For example, Aristotle argued that slaves are born rather than made and consequently, he turned the status of the slave into an inescapable fate (Heller and Fehér 1988: 16. These points all of course, tie in with Agnes Heller's analysis of the natural artifice of pre-modern arrangements; see Heller 1990).

However, Heller and Fehér argue that in the arrangements of modernity the existence of the individual is subjected to a fundamental reinterpretation. Whereas the pre-modern forms use notions of fate to explain and interpret the life chances and the meanings of individuality in the face of initial contingency, the modern forms typically involve another kind of explanation of the meaning of being thrown into the world. As Heller and Fehér put it, 'What had once been a fate, now becomes a context.' They continue to explain that from the modern point of view, 'if the accident of birth throws people into a context, instead of saddling them with the burden of fate, then neither the forms of life available, nor possibilities, are determined by birth' (Heller and Fehér 1988: 16).

For Heller and Fehér, this situation is to be embraced. They see it as a chance for the individual to escape any tendencies towards reification and instead, to become defining of her or his own life. They call this 'secondary contingency' and write that the individual 'becomes the bearer of possibilities or, to put it in a more extreme form, the individual becomes tantamount to his/her as yet undefined and undetermined possibilities. Everything becomes possible.' A little later, the point is repeated: 'The person is the maker of his/her life, and in this sense is a *self-made* man or a *self-made woman*' (Heller and Fehér 1988: 17).

Arguably, Huysmans' *Downstream* at the same time illustrates the strengths and weaknesses of the analysis of the modern contingency which is put forward by Agnes Heller and Ferenc Fehér. Certainly, Jean Folantin sees his life as something of his own making. That of course, is the root of his existential problem. Folantin is thrown back onto his own resources to carry out the pilgrimage for a satisfying meal. The route of the pilgrimage is determined by him in his own solitary walking. For Folantin, whilst the search amongst the restaurants of Paris lends a purpose and a context for life, the content of that life is self-defined. That content revolves around the sense of a lack and of a wanting which demands to be satisfied. But the quite unresolvable paradox is that if the content is filled then life itself will lose all meaning. It is precisely the discontent of civilization which makes Jean Folantin's life meaningful. Perhaps it is only the discontent which makes his life endurable. To this extent then, Jean Folantin is truly a self-made man. But of course, that is only part of the picture painted by Huysmans, and perhaps it is even the less interesting part at that.

The message of *Downstream* is one of the inescapable and desolate loneliness of being a self-made man in the metropolis of commodified exchange. The novel also stresses the impossibility of the achievement of self-constitution when all the individual has to rely on is him or her self. Moreover, Huysmans is keenly aware of the significance of the context of the erstwhile self-making. Rather unlike Heller and Fehér's sociology, his novels force the recognition that the context of the modern contingency is a physical and material, just as much as it is hermeneutic, fabrication. And the point is that the architecture of fabrication, the forms of the metropolitan existence, are themselves defining of life (such that, and as Benjamin pointed out, Haussmannization meant the disappearance of the self-defining contingency of the *flâneur* because it meant the demolition of the places to 'botanize on the asphalt' (Benjamin 1983).

Perhaps the perspective put forward by Agnes Heller and Ferenc Fehér demonstrates a kind of optical illusion. What they define as typical of modernity is in fact, nothing other than a revelation of the principles of their own post-modern condition. Indeed, the work of Heller and Fehér is so interesting precisely because they are so disturbed by the post-modernity which it is their destiny to live. On the one hand they appreciate the vantage point on modernity which is lent by the occupation of the spaces of post-modernity. But on the other hand, the vantage point merely confirms to them that modernity had many desirable aspects. What they interpret as typical of modernity is in fact, better understood as characteristic of post-modernity. For example, Heller and Fehér claim that in modernity it is 'not only the individual's relation to his/her initial "context" that becomes contingent; the context itself also becomes contingent. Put simply, from a modern point of view, particular social arrangements and institutions can just as well exist as not exist.' They continue: 'We can take the destiny of the world into our own hands. Just as our future depends on us, so too does the future of the world' (Heller and Fehér 1988: 17).

The comment might well be plausible (Heller and Fehér certainly think it is and they use it as the basis of a very laudable ethic for being in the world), but arguably it is only plausible as a description of the post-modern condition. From the modern point of view, it is emphatically not the case that institutions and arrangements need not exist. The kind of abyss of meaning which was identified by Franz Kafka in his story of the secret source of the authority of the law makes sure of that. Similarly for Jean Folantin, there simply had to be restaurants. His life was predicated on the necessary assumption that there simply had to be a good meal somewhere. For all those moderns who sought so desperately to make the world a better place, there simply had to be a linear time so that activities in the present could be consummated and redeemed by practices and arrangements in the future. The arrangements of the present could only be hermeneutically and historically justified through a nostalgia which simultaneously recalled a Golden Age of how good things used to be and how good they could be again. Quite simply, in the forms of modernity, the context of individuality simply does not become contingent. On the contrary, and as Huysmans' novel shows so well, it is subjected to tendencies towards reification which themselves transcend (or at least push under the carpet) the possibility of different arrangements.

It is only from a post-modern perspective that the arrangements and institutions of modernity come to seem to be contingent and therefore actually or potentially open to transcendence. Moreover, the analysis of contingency is not understood most keenly if it is seen as a description of modernity. Rather, the analysis of contingency is a more or less hesitant first step towards grasping the reflexivity of post-modernity.

It is in post-modernity that the context and meaning of individuality is recognized and practised as something which is contingent and not at all necessary. This is one of the insights contained in Michel Maffesoli's identification of the post-modern neo-tribalism. Maffesoli's point is, of course, that neo-tribes coalesce in post-modernity around the surface appearances of roles. Behind the surfaces, there are no fixed identities and no single historical destinies or trajectories. As opposed to the modern circumstances which hide or deny the significance of contingency, Maffesoli proposes that the post-modern condition accentuates con-tingency. For example, 'It is well understood that because the masses are perpetually seething, the tribes that crystallize within them are not stable: the people comprising the tribes are able to move from one tribe to another' (Maffesoli 1988: 141). In other words the groups, the tribes, which are the players on the social stage obey no necessity. They form, thrive and disappear simply through the contingent participation of the actors.

Moreover, according to Maffesoli, these actors are not to be understood as sovereign individuals who continuously and incrementally decide to be one thing today and something else tomorrow. (Huysmans' novels tend to show the problems and the possibilities which are contained in the modern construction of the sovereign individual. Huysmans shows that this individual might be an erstwhile creator and definer, but she or he is also desperately alone.) According to Michel Maffesoli: 'Individualism is an outdated bunker, one that deserves to be abandoned' (Maffesoli 1988: 144). He continues (through a very quick discussion of the plays of Samuel Beckett) to say that 'One recognizes here the persona, the mask that can be mutable and that, above all, integrates itself into a variety of scenes and situations whose relevance exists only because they are played out by many' (Maffesoli 1988: 144). Contingency is all.

In many ways, Maffesoli is providing an analysis of contingency which is compatible with the comments made by Agnes Heller and Ferenc Fehér. Yet he goes far beyond them. For Heller and Fehér, contingency is a largely ethical possibility. For them, the individual of modernity experiences and interprets the world as 'a "context", the context of our indeterminate possibilities'. It is within this context of the found world that the individual seeks to uphold an ethic of self-determination and thus, of the embracing of contingency (Heller and Fehér 1988: 29). Now, the problem with this argument is that the presupposition of the individual as a sovereign who is in principle able to be self-defining means that Heller and Fehér identify the individual as someone or something by way of a 'core' which is itself beyond the practices of the hermeneutic of contingency. The individual practises contingency without him or her self actually being contingent. Consequently, they tend to see the practices of self-definition as a kind of pilgrimage which is directed towards a largely ethical sense of satisfaction.

Heller and Fehér announce that they 'adopt the position, and the regard, of the contingent person who is intent on transforming his/her contingency into a destiny'. This transformation occurs for the individual, 'not through the satisfaction of mere wants, not even by detaching himself or herself from a context but by coping with the context while giving priority to the satisfaction of the needs of self-determination' (Heller and Fehér 1988: 30). Michel Maffesoli eschews this kind of commitment to destiny and instead emphasizes the contingency even of the individual. Whereas Heller and Fehér assume an individual who lives in contingency, Maffesoli assumes an individual persona which is itself contingent.

According to Maffesoli, neo-tribalism is not about satisfaction, destiny or self-definition. Rather, it is to be understood in terms of the playing out of roles in 'emotional communities' which are themselves thoroughly and wholly contingent. For example, Maffesoli argues that neo-tribalist groups are typified by fashion and display. They are exemplified by 'The diverse sights of "punk," "kiki," or "paninari," which nicely express the uniformity and conformity of these groups', and which 'offer specific instances of the ongoing spectacle generated by contemporary megalopolises' (Maffesoli 1988: 145). The individual does not come to these communities of the spectacle and the spectacular to seek satisfaction, rather she or he is shaped in these communities as a particular kind of feeling and experiencing subject. Put another way, we do not go to the restaurant from the street; it is the restaurant that makes us what we are. As post-modern individuals, we ourselves are contingent, as is our presence or absence at any particular restaurant (whereas Huysmans' Jean Folantin, as a modern individual, felt driven and compelled to visit different restaurants, the post-modern individuals will go for the décor or the celebrity rather than for the food).

Individuality is practised in constitutive communities rather than co-operative communities. Consequently, Maffesoli's concepts of sociality and neo-tribalism seek to grasp a multifaceted and all-encompassing contingency: 'In its various forms, neo-tribalism refuses to be identified with specific political endeavors, does not conform to any single definite structure, and has as its sole *raison d'être* the preoccupation with the collectively lived present' (Maffesoli 1988: 146). In other words, neo-tribalism intimates a kind of nomad-like situation and significantly, the immortality of the ever-recurring reflexive present.

Of course, it would be inappropriate to deny the important differences over the ontology of contingency which can be easily seen between Heller and Fehér on the one hand and Michel Maffesoli on the other. However, it is nevertheless noticeable that to some extent, the pictures they paint of the post-modern condition look rather similar in places (that is, assuming the suggestion that Heller and Fehér's work operates in terms of an optical illusion is actually accepted). They share an emphasis on the recognition (rather than on the modern refusal) of contingency and moreover, they are concerned to place the practices and interests of self-definition at the centre of the analytic stage. The difference is that whereas Heller and Fehér identify self-definition as definition by the self, Michel Maffesoli identifies it as a ceaseless process of the definition of the self. Moreover, whilst Heller and Fehér suppose that the self-definition has a goal and purpose of satisfaction, Maffesoli sees it as lacking any goal other than transient participation in communities of feeling (which presumably to some considerable extent bear comparison with the aesthetic communities of Immanuel Kant).

But there is another much more implicit point of agreement between Heller and Fehér and Maffesoli. Both of the approaches presuppose the ability of individuals to be self-sufficiently defining of themselves. They take it for granted that the individuals are possessed of the moral, hermeneutic and significantly, the material resources to be able to practise all the self-definition they want. In other words, in so far as the post-modern condition does indeed revolve around a perception and an experience of reflexivity, so it is also predicated on the taken for granted presence of the resources which will enable reflexivity. Put more simply, post-modernity presupposes a post-scarcity economy (here I am using the word 'economy' in a rather general sense somewhat after Foucault; it implies more than just the technical sphere which is called the 'economic'. Instead, it implies all the milieux and spheres of production, consumption, distribution and exchange. In this sense then, it is perfectly possible to speak of a moral economy or a hermeneutic economy).

Post-modernity involves acts and practices of self-definition and reflexivity. Consequently it is only possible to the extent that the resources of self-definition are already and relatively readily available. For example, I can only choose to dress in one way as opposed to another (in Maffesoli's terms, I can only participate in this network of the post-modern sociality) to the extent that, firstly, I possess accurate information about the symbolism and the cultural meanings of different codes of dress, secondly, I have the money or the wherewithal to be able to have access to the necessary clothes and, thirdly, that I possess the resources (which might well revolve around physical attributes as much as social and cultural ones) which will enable me to be accepted by the host community. Much the same trinity of post-scarcity is also required if I am participating in moral and hermeneutic economies. To be a persona which is constituted in the post-modern social and cultural groups is firstly to be able to choose from amongst a multitude of goods.

The presumption of the ability to choose, and indeed, the presumption of the availability of the chosen resources, seems to be simply taken for granted by the commentators of contingency. However, it is arguably the case that the involvement of the post-modern social and cultural groups in a post-scarcity economy has profound moral implications. The implications revolve around the relationships between the post-modern and the modern. (Remember, I am not at all arguing that post-modernity is a universal condition. I am simply suggesting that it is a condition occupied and demonstrated by those groups who practise a reflexive deconstruction of their own conditions of existence. Where there is post-modernity, there too is modernity.)

As such, the most important point of conflict which arises with the emergence of post-modernity is not interior to that condition (even though there are conflicts between different neo-tribes; these conflicts are temporary in comparison to the exterior line of conflict). As and where it is possible to identify the post-modern condition, so the most important line of conflict is that between the post-modern and the modern. On the one hand, the post-modern groups are operating and practising the nomad-like activity of reflexive self-definition in a milieu of abundance (or at least of enough) whereas, and on the other hand, the modern groups are operating in terms of a pilgrim-like activity in a milieu of want and scarcity.

The struggle of the pilgrim-like quest of modernity only occurs because of the perception, or real existence, of scarcity in the present. After all, it is only because of scarcity, and in order to make good a want, that a pilgrimage, a journey from here to there, is carried out in the first place. The pilgrimage-like activity implies some actual or sensed need on the part of social and cultural groups or individuals which is quite incapable of satisfaction in the present. But the post-modern nomad-like activity is predicated on the abundance of resources in the present. The groups of post-modernity can in principle satisfy every want and therefore, they quite lack any purpose in linear time. They do not need to struggle to satisfy their wants since the resources of satisfaction are simply supposed to be available in the here and now (not least, thanks to the technology which, in a kind of Faustian pact, satisfies previously unimagined wants and desires at the expense of the ever greater removal of technology from the orbit of social and cultural intervention).

Maffesoli to some extent realizes that precisely because of the post-scarcity economy, post-modernity is typified by a restlessness which however, never gets anywhere (precisely because there is nowhere, no single place, to go to). Maffesoli comments that 'The jogger, the punk, the retro-look, the bon-chic-bon-genre, the street entertainers, all invite us into a world of incessant movement' (Maffesoli 1988: 148). But, and this is the point which Maffesoli does not adequately emphasize, these figures of the city also invite us into a world of plenty. Those groups or individuals which continue to want, and which identify themselves and are identified by others in terms of the longevity of that want (that is, those groups or individuals which are interpreted and understood in terms of fixed identities) are quite incapable of participation as equals in the world of post-modernity.

If post-modernity is predicated on abundance, then it is also the case that the post-scarcity milieu can only be maintained through the deliberate refusal to accept the claims to inclusion of others. The post-modernity of certain social groups is only sustainable at the expense of the perpetual entrapment in conditions of scarcity of other groups of potential competitors. Put another way, the post-modern condition can only reproduce its immortal consumptions in so far as the necessary mortal production is reproduced by those who are kept outside.

However, even if the modern groups are not successfully excluded from post-modernity, it is improbable that they are capable of entering into the pointless cornucopia on their own accord. More or less by definition, the groups which continue to uphold the identities of want and therefore of pilgrimage cannot possibly become post-modern. Of course, this inability is due in a large part to the logical impossibility of the achievement of the pilgrimage-like quest. But it is also due to the fundamental non-contingency of the pilgrims themselves. Basically, some social and cultural groups are always and perhaps even inevitably trapped in scarcity. These groups are so tightly defined by reification of one sort or another that there is little or no space to allow even the merest glimmer of a chance that they might be or might become reflexively self-defining.

It is possible to identify two main grounds for the imprisonment within scarcity. They can be called the material and the stigmatic. Each deserves a little investigation.

When he tries to identify typical post-modern tribes, Michel Maffesoli tends to talk about the urban types of the jogger or the street entertainer. The point is that these kinds of tribes are in control of their urban environment. For them, the city has become a taken for granted home, a second nature, to such an extent that it can either be a running track (but who are the spectators? who are the athletes?) or a stage (but who are the performers? who are the audience?). But the city is also inhabited by groups who are not in control of their urban environment. These groups tend to lack the resources to make their environment what they will. Instead they tend to experience it as a dull compunction. These groups, which are typified by the figures of the homeless and the poor, are materially imprisoned within their needs. These groups are trapped on the very cutting edge of scarcity. They are not seeking to satisfy socially constructed wants, they are seeking to satisfy physically imposed needs.

The poor and the homeless are materially incapable of post-modernity for themselves, by their own acts of self-definition (however much they might impinge upon the consciousness of the post-modern, but perhaps they actually do not impinge too much except when they are background figures in pop videos) for reasons which have been known since Marx and Engels. After all, and as Marx and Engels so correctly pointed out in *The German Ideology*, 'Men must be in a position to live in order to be able to "make history" '. They continue: 'But life involves before everything else eating and drinking, a habitation, clothing and many other things' (Marx and Engels 1970: 48). In this sense, it might even be possible to propose that the urban poor and homeless have been pushed into a pre-historical and a pre-modern stage in so far as it is by no means self-evident that they are able to satisfy the needs of material life. Here then, the post-modern condition lives side by side with the pre-modern as well as the modern. Indeed and by extension, it would rather seem that the conditions of post-history, history and pre-history are simultaneous.

The pilgrims of poverty simply cannot practise reflexivity. Even less are they in the condition of contingency suggested by Heller and Fehér. This is simply because they are, on the contrary, in the condition of direct material need. Consequently they cannot produce their own definitions of their own existence. As Frederick Engels said in his speech at the graveside of Marx, 'mankind must first of all eat and drink, have shelter and clothing, before it can pursue politics, science, religion, art, etc.' (Engels 1942: 16). It is to say the least, unfortunate that so much of the literature on post-modernity has evidently lost sight of this so simple and so telling point. The tragedy and the ethical problem of post-modernity is how the post-modern groups can come to terms with that pre-history of some of the other urban inhabitants, a pre-history which the post-modern groups have a direct interest in maintaining.

That is of course, assuming that the post-modern groups want to come to terms with the continuation of the pre-historical and the historical. It is by no means self-evident that they either do or can. In many ways, the precondition of their contingency and certainly the precondition of the availability of the material resources of contingency is precisely the want of those resources amongst others. To a very considerable extent, it might even be said that it is exactly the inability of the poor and homeless to practise art, politics and all the other forms of self-creation, which provides the invariant benchmark by which contingency can be known as contingency. I am self-defining, and know myself to be so, precisely because I can look at those others and see what life is like when it is reified as material need. Without them, I might not know myself to be like a kind of nomad who can flit from tribe to tribe in an endless and thoroughly circular orgy of consumption. Their existence in the face of dull compunction and reification helps constitute my creativity and reflexivity. It is their position outside of the post-modern which makes it possible to know what the insides are like.

Indeed, the lot of the poor and homeless as the others on the outside of the post-modern condition is exacerbated since they are also subjects of the second form of the imprisonment within scarcity. Along with numerous other groups, the poor and the homeless are imprisoned within the fruitless struggle of pilgrimage-like activities and identities through strategies of stigmatization. Through this stigmatization certain social and cultural groups are marked as disgraceful, flawed, inadequate and therefore as passive objects of the attribution of meaning, rather than as the subjects of the creation of meaning in their own right.

The sociological significance of stigma has been explored most originally by Erving Goffman. Goffman shows that stigma is attached to those individuals, groups or attributes which are defined as discreditable from the point of view of 'normal' expectations. He begins his analysis with the methodological point that 'Society establishes the means of categorizing persons and the complement of attributes felt to be ordinary and natural for members of each of these categories. Social settings establish the categories of persons likely to be encountered there' (Goffman 1968: 11–12). Goffman makes the basis of stigma quite clear when he says that: 'A stigma, then, is really a special kind of relationship between attribute and stereotype' (Goffman 1968: 14).

Goffman's analysis leads to the thesis that from the point of view of those who look towards post-modernity as the basis of the classifications of the normal (normal both in terms of the expectations of social relationships and of the attributes of the participants), the social and the societal is based upon material or hermeneutic abundance. The social settings of post-modernity emphasize the contingency of choice in the market place of goods, ideas or styles. All of these things are interpreted as commodities to be consumed rather than simply as material resources which can satisfy material needs. The post-modern market places are supposed normally to be occupied only by those who are able to choose and who are able to define their lives for themselves, quite free of any kind of reification. Consequently, any groups or individuals which are interpreted as possessing discreditable attributes (attributes which invariably imply reification) are stigmatized from the point of view of post-modernity. They are excluded from the realms of post-modern normalcy (to say the least, it is exceedingly rare to find a beggar in a shopping mall). They are thus defined and therefore rendered non-contingent.

The possession of certain attributes such as poverty is an occasion for stigmatization and that stigmatization reinforces the inability of that group to enter into post-modernity. They are stuck in an almost seamless and inescapable double-bind of inadequacy. 'He is thus reduced in our minds from a whole and usual person to a tainted, discounted one. Such an attribute is a stigma . . . It constitutes a special discrepancy between virtual and actual social identity' (Goffman 1968: 13).

The importance of stigma, and its effect on the possibilities of the social participation of the stigmatized, has also been explored by Susan Sontag. In her work on the metaphorical construction of the AIDS virus, Sontag clearly owes debts to Goffman (debts which she acknowledges). But she manages to make profound insights of her own. In particular, she shows how the metaphors which surround the AIDS virus lead to the stigmatization of the person with AIDS. Consequently, Susan Sontag provides something by way of a case study in the construction of non-contingency and therefore, of exclusion and inadequacy for post-modernity. But, given that she is talking about something which might strike anyone who does not take due care and attention (and the research seems to indicate that actually not many of us do take such care), Sontag also helps develop a realization that the status of the individual as a post-modern participant is not once and for all. Quite the contrary, post-modernity is potentially revocable. Or, put another way and rather more bluntly, the terminally ill are thrown out of the situations of post-modernity. Their illness defines them as non-contingent and therefore, as abnormal from the perspective of the prerequisites for the participation in post-modernity (hence once again, enhancing the immortality of those on the 'inside').

Given that post-modernity fundamentally stresses self-definition and reflexivity, AIDS is an especially serious hermeneutic, moral and personal problem. It imposes identities and meanings on the individual. The person who has AIDS is socially stigmatized as a certain (and therefore as a reified) kind of individual who had been trying to hide the truth of their existence. AIDS implies a fixed identity. And that stigmatization means that any and all practices of self-definition are dismissed as little more than illicit glosses on a deeper lack of contingency. Sontag puts it all much more clearly. She writes that 'The illness flushes out an identity that might have remained hidden from neighbors, jobmates, family, friends' (Sontag 1991: 110). According to Sontag, 'Indeed, to get AIDS is precisely to be revealed, in the majority of cases so far, as a member of a certain "risk group", a community of pariahs' (Sontag 1991: 110). And to be a member of a 'risk group' is to be defined; it is not at all to be the defining subject of one's own contingency. 'AIDS is understood in a premodern way ... which also revives the archaic idea of a tainted community that illness has judged' (Sontag 1991: 132). Not least, that judgement consists in imputations of reification.

Despite their other very important differences, the poor and the AIDS patients can be seen as having one thing in common other than their stigmatization. They are also like social and secular pilgrims. The poor and the homeless are after the pre-requisites for history (whereas the post-modern groups already have everything to hand). Meanwhile, AIDS patients are also like pilgrims. But their pilgrimage is of a double-headed kind; either they are like pilgrims on the road of mortality or they are like pilgrims on the road of technological progress. They too are going somewhere.

Now, I am not saying that AIDS and poverty are the only areas which illustrate the problem of the line of division and conflict between modernity and post-modernity. Neither am I saying that other contexts of the post-modern practises of stigmatization and non-contingency are unimportant (for example, gender and race are extremely important issues. For an especially useful discussion of the relationship between gender and post-modernity, see Nicholson 1990). I am more modestly proposing that the issues of the poor and the AIDS patients are particularly telling illustrations of a general series of dilemmas and difficulties. Primarily, the difficulties are of a moral kind. They revolve around the question of the nature of the relationship between the post-modern and the modern and even, quite probably, the pre-modern. The post-modern, modern and pre-modern tend to occupy very different cultural, material and hermeneutic milieux but spatially they tend to be remarkably close neighbours (as anyone who has walked along a few streets in London since the early 1980s should know full well). The question is one of how that contradiction can be resolved and how it might be that these different milieux might be able to live together. But given that it is the post-modern which has the big guns of moral, material and hermeneutic abundance under its control, the difficulty is largely one for it to ponder.

Arguably, the post-modern social and cultural groups can come to terms with the existence of the pre-modern and the modern others through either of three strategies. They can opt for either annihilation of the others, for toleration or for what Richard Rorty has dubbed 'liberal ironism' (Rorty 1989). In modern conditions, a fourth option might have been viable; the option of assimilation. However, in the conditions of post-modernity, assimilation is not a realistic option for a variety of reasons. Firstly, and most obviously, the 'outsiders' with their pilgrim-like identities lack the resources which would enable them to sustain and reproduce their erstwhile post-modernity. Secondly, such a granting of post-modernity would actually reinforce stigma ('we had to give them things; they were incapable of getting the things for themselves'). Thirdly, assimilation is impossible simply because there is no solid and transcendental core of the post-modern identity to be assimilated to. More or less by definition, post-modern identities change with a remarkable speed and frequency (or at least, they can change that way in principle) and therefore, any assimilation will quickly become outdated and redundant.

Moreover, to the extent that the post-modern groups actually cannot practise the physical annihilation of the pre-modern and the modern others (not least because it is the others who in large measure generate the resources of the post-scarcity economy of abundance and contingency), and of course to the extent that annihilation is a very long way from being a moral course of action, the problem of the others can only be dealt with through the last two options of toleration and liberal ironism.

The meanings and limitations of toleration have been usefully explored by Susan Mendus. In her splendid essay, *Toleration and the Limits of Liberalism*, Mendus makes the point that toleration is typically an issue in social, cultural and moral situations which are characterized by diversity. The situation is one in which each group sees practices and attitudes which it disapproves of and yet must learn to live with. In other words, toleration is an issue in moral contexts where neither annihilation nor assimilation are held to be legitimate or perhaps even desirable options. However, toleration also implies a positive act of letting be; it implies that one group could change the activities of the others if it chose and yet it chooses not to. As Susan Mendus suggests, 'the circumstances of toleration are circumstances in which there is diversity coupled with disapproval, dislike, or disgust, and where the tolerator has the power to influence the tolerated' (Mendus 1989: 20).

Here, Mendus is making a claim which resonates very much with the post-modern condition which I have been trying to sketch. It is indeed the case that the post-modern social and cultural groups disapprove of, or are disgusted by, the existence of the denizens of pre-history and history (that is, the post-modern are more or less disgusted by the pre-modern and the modern). It is also the case that the post-modern groups could if they so wished influence the pre-modern and the modern. For example, it is possible in purely practical terms to either house all the homeless or to 'tidy up' the streets of London by shipping all the homeless somewhere else. But, and as Mendus stresses, there is a 'paradox of toleration' which revolves around the difficulty of 'how the tolerator might think it good to tolerate that which is morally wrong' (Mendus 1989: 20).

It is at this point that Mendus' argument possibly ceases to apply to the post-modern moral situation. Quite simply, Mendus assumes that the tolerator actually notices the activities and practices which are held to be wrong or inappropriate. However, it is doubtful that this is actually the case. Indeed, it seems to be more reasonable to suggest that the post-modern groups let the pre-modern and the modern be simply because those on the outside are not noticed. They are simply not identified from the post-modern point of view as subjects who make pressing moral claims.

Consequently, the homeless are left to live and die on the streets of London because, firstly, they are not identified as part of the same world (perhaps for the first time in human history, post-modernity means that the simultaneous occupation of geographical space does not imply the simultaneous occupation of moral and societal space. The city walls mentioned by Hans Jonas have been indeed transcended by some). The homeless are members of a different historical universe. Secondly, the homeless are not noticed because they are denied a face. All that is seen by the post-modern spectator is a huddle of rags and filth or an excuse for a better burglar alarm (here then, the homeless and the destitute are taken as an intimation of a return to the state of nature of Hobbes). Susan Sontag has written that 'Our very notion of the person, of dignity, depends on the separation of face from body, on the possibility that the face may be exempt, or exempt itself, from what is happening to the body' (Sontag 1991: 126). But if the face is reduced to the status of an expression of the body, or if it is just not seen at all, then the faceless becomes a non-person and a profoundly undignified mass. (The ethical importance of the face is also stressed by Emmanuel Levinas. See Levinas 1988: 168–80.)

Basically, then, the post-modern is or might well be, tolerant more or less by default of the pre-modern and the modern simply because those expressions of reification and want are not noticed and are certainly not constructed as relevant. As such, the letting be and possibly even the plurality of post-modernity is not necessarily a sign of a benevolent acceptance of diversity, self-definition and individual autonomy (it is not self-evidently a measure of the emergence of an ethical shell for the imperatives emphasized by the likes of Heller and Fehér). Quite the contrary, it might well be a demonstration of moral, hermeneutic and societal myopia.

Perhaps Rorty's pragmatics of liberal ironism is a better way of understanding the implication of the existence of disdained others on the post-modern. Rorty explains what liberal ironism means by splitting the phrase into its two parts. He says that 'liberals are people who think that cruelty is the worst thing we do.' Meanwhile, an ironist is 'the sort of person who faces up to the contingency of his or her own most central beliefs and desires.' Consequently, and bringing together these two definitions, Richard Rorty proposes that 'Liberal ironists are people who include among these ungroundable desires their own hope that suffering will be diminished, that the humiliation of human beings by other human beings may cease' (Rorty 1989: xv). In other words, liberal ironism involves a moral commitment to the reduction of cruelty but also the knowledge that there is no transcendental basis for that reduction. Liberal ironism is a mode of ethical subjectivity which knows itself to be contingent on circumstances of time, place and particularly importantly for Rorty, vocabulary.

Now Rorty's suggestions might well be a useful way of overcoming the divide and the point of conflict between post-modernity and everything else. Certainly, Rorty's approach remains appropriate to the status and nature of the inhabitants of post-modernity. He does seem to offer a basis upon which it is possible for the post-modern social and cultural groups to look out to and to identify the others as relevant. To this extent, Rorty's liberal ironism might well be a desirable attitude. But its practical implications seem rather limited.

The point is that the liberal ironist desires a decrease of the humiliation of human beings and of the cruelty visited upon them, but that is to presuppose that poverty for example actually is held to be a humiliation. Of course, I am not saying that poverty is not a humiliation, but it is by no means self-evident that poverty is an offence to liberal ironism. For example, according to some philosophers and economists (invariably astonishingly wealthy ones) poverty is a very edifying condition. For them, it is not a humiliation (or at least, if it is a humiliation it is also a very good thing indeed since it leads to a recommitment to hard work and enterprise).

As such, if liberal ironism is one of the only ways in which the post-modern can forge moral links with, and recognize the moral relevance of the pre-modern and the modern, then it implies an enhancement of contingency. After all, liberal ironism is at heart nothing other than a choice; I only see poverty as humiliating because I choose to do so. And the basis of that choice is a leap of imagination on my part. There is nothing necessary about it. That is why Rorty spends so long talking about novels rather than about philosophy. According to him, it is through novels that it is possible to make the imaginative connections which are the basis of a human solidarity which has to be consciously made. Novels are the tools of imagination and therefore of transcendence. Human solidarity is not, by this reading, something which is waiting to be found. It is something which has to be made on the basis of an effort to see all others as in some way like me. Rorty's liberal ironism is 'the ethnocentrism of a "we" ("we liberals") which is dedicated to enlarging itself, to creating an ever larger and more variegated *ethnos*. It is the "we" of the people who have been brought up to distrust ethnocentrism' (Rorty 1989: 198).

As Rorty says, and perhaps this is all the inhabitant of post-modernity can say by way of an ethical imperative: 'We should stay on the lookout for marginalized people – people who we still instinctively think of as "they" rather than "us". We should try to notice our similarities with them' (Rorty 1989: 196). But the sociological pressures and tendencies of the post-modern condition seem to imply that 'we' will not notice 'our' similarities with 'them'. After all, 'we' do not really know who 'we' are anymore. It is even questionable whether 'I' know who 'I' am. That is also the mark of contingency.

Chapter 7

Conclusion

This book has been constructed around the development of an initial premise and the consequent implication of a thesis. The premise represents an attempt to work in terms of the narrative of the conflict in modern culture which was identified by Georg Simmel (and which I then identified as something of a common theme in the representative statements of modernity). I have been trying to suggest that if Simmel's story of the conflict between form and life is rendered more fully sociological (not least through the re-interpretation of the mysterious quality called life) and if instead, it is interpreted as a conflict between a reflexive will to know and a will to certainty which rather more tends towards reification, then it becomes possible to provide some kind of explanation of the stakes and the evident features of post-modernity. However, it should be stressed that the account of post-modernity which I have offered should be treated as a story of post-modernity. It does not at all pretend to the status of being the story.

The thesis which emerges out of this premise is that post-modernity cannot really be understood as a fully fledged condition in its own right. Quite the contrary. If post-modernity is one expression of a conflict of modernity and if, moreover, post-modernity is therefore a point of critique of modernity which is nevertheless dependent on modernity, then it is the case that post-modernity is a condition of transcendence. In itself, it has little or nothing by way of a set of definite, characteristic features. It is simply an overcoming of institutions, arrangements and relationships which were elevated to the status of a second nature through the reifying tendencies of modernity.

But modernity had to betray tendencies towards reification. Those tendencies represented so many more or less desperate attempts to hide away the abyss of meaning which is a possibility in the wake of the deconstruction of natural artifice. And the point was precisely that the abyss of meaning indeed had to be avoided at all costs if life was to be existentially and hermeneutically possible. As such, I propose that post-modernity, and the post-modern condition, can only be understood dialectically and in terms of all of those modern things which it attempts reflexively to deconstruct and overcome.

In rather more concrete hermeneutic terms, this means that post-modernity can be taken as the intimation of a transcendence of all the modern establishments of universality. The simultaneous existence of the pre-historical, the historical and the post-historical conditions means that the erstwhile universality of the modern imaginations and categories (such as Society or Progress) have been challenged in the most fundamental ways. It is no longer at all self-evident (if indeed it ever was) that all the subjects and citizens of a single Society can be understood by reference to the same universal criteria. After all, imaginations like Society are about nothing so much as the identification and practical implementation of exclusive bounded communities. The imagination of Society invariably tends to involve an equation of the community of social reciprocity with specific geographical areas. As such it tends to establish an internally homogeneous 'us' in opposition to an externally heterogeneous 'them'; friends in opposition to enemies. But some of the intimations of post-modernity mean precisely that these universals are undermined. The heterogeneous moves inside from the outside and all the fixed identities which universal imaginations presuppose seemingly are made fluid. Instead, the universal imaginations and standards have evidently been subsumed by the particular. But these particulars only possess whatever features and force they do in so far as they feed off and challenge the ostensibly universal products of modernity.

Even though some specific styles or attitudes might be labelled post-modern (if only for the want of any other suitable label), it is nevertheless the case that post-modernity as a social and a cultural universe is in itself, largely nothing. It is certainly not The Great Transformation in social and cultural arrangements which some of the enthusiasts claim it to be.

Perhaps the premise and the thesis go a very long way indeed towards explaining why this book actually says so much about the difficulties and contradictions of modernity but so little about post-modernity itself. Indeed, despite its declared intentions and subject matter, the story I have told seems to permanently skirt around the problem of post-modernity without actually approaching it. But perhaps that is largely inevitable. To talk about post-modernity is to talk about a series of absences and transcendences. To the extent that post-modernity reflects and represents a dialectical conflict at the very heart of modernity (indeed a conflict which is in many ways the essence of modernity, or which at least was frequently the pivotal dilemma of some of the finest reflections of modernity), it can only be understood and interpreted by reference to what has happened to the modern forms and arrangements.

But this creates and implies yet another problem. It revolves around the extent to which post-modernity implies the redundancy of sociology as an intellectual discipline. This area of difficulty might also mean the redundancy of sociology as a way of opening up the roads to freedom (but roads which cannot be mapped prior to the journey along them).

The point seems to be this. Sociology as a discipline of hermeneutic investigation and reflexivity is predicated upon the ability to say something about the social and the societal milieux. And that saying (that attempt to answer the question, 'what happened?') presupposes, if not actively requires, an orderly and therefore a bounded set of meanings and possibilities. For example, it is only possible to develop a discourse about some entity which is called 'society', in so far as it is possible to imagine a bounded milieu of relationships which stands more or less in isolation from any other imagined milieu called 'society'. To some extent, it is only possible to know of the relationships and processes of say, German 'society' because of the difference of that bounded universe from the other universe which is called French 'society'.

But post-modernity is fundamentally and intrinsically the transcendence of boundaries. It represents so many hermeneutic, material and moral enterprises of the going beyond of the entities called forth in the modern imaginations and practices. As such, post-modernity essentially means an attempt to go beyond the preconditions of the sociological discourse. It means a transcendence of the promises and possibilities of sociology itself.

Of course, to many people, that might well seem to be one of the least pressing of the myriad difficulties which post-modernity might imply. When all is said and done, perhaps there is some validity to the possible comment that reflections on the future of sociology are of a fairly minor significance compared with say, famine and technological disaster. But, in many ways what happens to sociology might well be symptomatic of what happens to social and cultural relationships, to social and cultural efforts in self-definition.

The point is that even though it has often been remarkably unsuccessful and tedious, sociology is about the explanation of the world. It is fundamentally predicated on the thesis that social and cultural events can be explained and understood in social and cultural terms. Sociology revels in the stark and cold belief that, despite tendencies which might imply the contrary, men and women actually can be sufficient unto themselves. The world can be what we will it to be; but that also means that there are no excuses for us.

Consequently, to practise sociology is, or perhaps it is better to say that it can be, an exercise in the multiplication of social and cultural possibilities. If I know why an event happened, I might also be able to say that it did not need to happen, or that other things might happen in the future. I am multiplying the meanings of the world and therefore I am creating freedom. But all of that requires that it is possible to call forth some bounded milieu or perhaps more importantly, some fixed identities, against which is it possible to know 'what happened?' And it is precisely those constitutions of the knowing which post-modernity challenges.

Yet in its turn that might well mean that the terrain of the post-modern sociality ceases to be something which can be explained. If sociology is impossible so might freedom and reflexivity be impossible as well.

So far, I have spoken about the implications of post-modernity for what might be called 'interpretive sociology'. But post-modernity also means serious things for what might, by contrast, be called 'legislative sociology' (for an exploration of the differences between the interpretive and the legislative modes, see Bauman 1987). Sociology has such a deep involvement in the assumptions and self-images of modernity precisely because with its categories of 'society' and 'order' and so forth it could generate the hermeneutic resources which made it possible for the abyss of meaning to be avoided. The avoidance took the form of the identification of erstwhile social and societal laws and regularities. The identified regularities were restricted to specific bounded milieux and were supposed to step into the voids left by the deconstruction of natural artifice. In these terms then, it might even be said that the modern sociology was possessed of the ability to become the deity of the disenchanted culture (but it was only possessed of the ability; one of the most interesting stories of modernity will centre around the discovery of precisely why and how sociology, and more significantly the sociologists themselves, proved to be so amazingly and consistently inept in establishing themselves as the new providers of value. Was it because the pronouncement of the evident ability of sociology was not made loudly enough? Or was it because the sociologists either were not believed or were not very good at shouting?).

Whether interpretive or legislative, the modern sociology sought to reflect and understand events which had taken place already. Indeed and thanks to the assurances of linear time, sociology was also taken to be able

to identify the events which really ought to take place in the
created new meanings of the world by explaining the pre
to a past and a future. Moreover, the essentially d'
sociological knowledge and truth played no small pa
hermeneutic activity to the interests of reflexivity. The point about sociology
is precisely that, notwithstanding the apparent confidence and certainty of the
sociologists and their productions, absolute agreement is impossible within
the discipline. The impossibility reflects the fact that sociology is not a God's
eye enterprise (regardless of the so many claims to the contrary). Rather, and
as Steven Lukes has shown so well and so simply, the practice of sociology
involves also buying into moral, philosophical and historical package deals
which might well be mutually wholly incommensurable (perhaps this is also
one of the points which the otherwise somewhat polarized 'two sociologies'
picture tries to grasp. See Lukes 1981).

Even more than all of this, and arguably despite the frequent vacuity
or plain irrelevance of the claims, the declarations of the scientificity of
sociology meant that the enterprise was also being harnessed to the
vocational trajectory established by Max Weber. As well as moral and
ontological incommensurability then, sociology was also put on a train of
the gradual upsetting of all the certainties which had previously been
established by sociology (much the same was implied if sociology was
connected to a more philosophical destiny of Enlightenment. As Kant
saw the matter, Enlightenment fundamentally means that nothing must be
taken for granted; and that logically includes the earlier successes of the
Enlightenment itself; see Kant 1970).

Certainly sociology was consequently built upon intellectual, hermeneutic and historical foundations which were to say the least, pulling in a
variety of directions. The discipline was, is and will hopefully remain,
fundamentally unstable. But despite these complex and important
disagreements, it is nevertheless possible to generalize a little. It is not too
inappropriate to suggest that modern sociology is built upon two positions
which have been nicely expressed by Jean François Lyotard (even though
he is talking about something else, art. But perhaps sociology and art are
aesthetically, not too different. See Lyotard 1984. I have tried to say a
little about the aesthetics of modern sociology in Tester 1992a).

Even though he is not, Lyotard could well be unravelling one of the
central assumptions of sociology when he says that this 'thought seizes
upon what is received, it seeks to determine what has already been
thought, written, painted, or socialized in order to determine what hasn't
been' (Lyotard 1984: 37). If this statement is applied to sociology, it
implies, perfectly reasonably, that sociology talks about the 'real world

of everyday existence' (or whatever other ontological referents might be offered) precisely to show that things do not have to be this way. Specifically, this invariably means for the modern sociological narratives that there is an assumption that the prevailing, existent arrangements are somewhat worse than they otherwise might be. Things might be improved. Although the meanings of improvement will vary depending on whether the sociological enterprise is legislative or reflexive (that is, depending on whether it is pursued in the interests of a will to certainty or of a will to know), and depending on the moral package deals which the sociologist buys into, it will be nevertheless shown through a seizing on 'what is received' that things could be better than they are.

This first position leads to the second one. If it is accepted that some possible things have not taken place, or that some possibilities have not yet been realized (the usual unrealized possibility is of course, The Great Proletarian Revolution), then it is also the case that it is impossible to say the very last thing about the social and the societal (of course, the status of these counterfactuals is by no means clear. From a sociological point of view it would seem reasonable to propose that the truth content of the counterfactuals is dependent upon the hermeneutic and the moral critique which is made of the existing arrangements; their truth is generated by the prior concern about the actual).

Lyotard is making the claim that any definitive answer to the question of 'what happened?' is impossible to unravel. If a reflection on the real and the existent generates an awareness that something else might pertain, then it is simply impossible to say the last word because the last word will be located after the something else has actually taken place. But even that last word cannot be said. After all, there is always an existent and therefore, there is always a something else. Perhaps he is guilty of making a broad generalization but Lyotard nevertheless makes an important statement when he comments that: 'All intellectual disciplines and institutions take for granted that not everything has been said, written, or recorded, that words already heard or pronounced are not the last words' (Lyotard 1984: 37).

The point is however, that this recognition of the possibility of different arrangements, different events, different worlds, is only sustainable if firstly, it is possible to identify something about which it can be said that 'it happened' (that is, to the extent that it is possible to apply categories which enable the presentation to the understanding of an event) and secondly, it is possible to develop some imagination or some representation of an alternative. In other words, and to apply all of this to the enterprise of modern sociology, it can only explain the existent and

only call forth another better world if it can constitute and iden.
boundaries which give place, meaning and direction to the 'what'
happens'. Indeed, sociology can only be critical of this world (that is, it
can only say that 'this is bad' but, if it is so chosen, avoid legislating the
meaning of what is therefore taken to be 'good') if it can look at
constituted boundaries from a position somewhat without their bounds.

In relation to modernity, post-modernity offers precisely that
possibility. In other words, the post-modern baby should not be thrown
out with the bath water. Without some imagination of something called
post-modernity it would be more or less impossible to develop any kind
of understanding of modernity. Post-modernity is the transcendence of
boundaries. As such, modernity becomes a condition which can be
explored and interpreted. But post-modernity, or at least the non-critical
and over-enthusiastic occupation of post-modern spaces has other
implications which might be rather less than entirely desirable.

Quite simply, if post-modernity is the intimation of a transcendent
condition without the bounds of modernity then, consequently, it is also
the intimation of a condition in which questions of the status of what has
or has not happened become quite beyond the asking. After all, post-
modernity means a transcendence of the boundaries which constitute the
basis of any knowing of what might be (without the boundaries it is
distinctly possible that there can be no understanding). As such,
post-modernity as transcendence of modern boundaries implies a
condition in which the existent cannot be explained or interpreted. It can
only be confronted as a simple and an unalterable fact. In the post-modern
condition, the existent is without bounds (after all, there are no bounds for
it to be within; no bounds to contain it). A situation is intimated in which
the existent might swamp and perpetually escape any and every attempt
to represent and understand it. It is a dull fact about which it might well
be hermeneutically impossible to allow for any alternative.

Consequently, in so far as post-modernity pushes the social and the
cultural beyond the social and societal understanding, so the social and
the cultural might also be beyond the social and the societal interference.
And that is actually tantamount to saying that post-modernity intimates
nothing other than the construction of a new natural artifice. It might
betray a tendency towards a denial of human freedom. It is certainly a
refusal to face up to the full consequences of freedom (but it has been
known, albeit for extremely different reasons, since Kant and the
existentialists, that for some the abrogation of freedom might be a very
attractive proposition indeed. Freedom is not easy, and neither is it
necessarily very pleasant. But it is the most we can have).

...ondition implies a mere ability to register and
...t without any chance of the legitimate posing of the
...It is in other words, a rendering of the existent as a
...fact and quite without any meaning other than the
...ction of its being.

...gy which retains a commitment to the enterprises, lessons
an... ...of modernity is simply overwhelmed by the intimations of
post-m... ...nity. But any sociology which gives up on the problems and
possibilities of modernity and which instead, attempts to deal head on
with the post-modern condition and contingency, ceases to be able to
make any judgement whatsoever. It is instead, reduced to the level of a
simple and a more or less insignificant description. Empiricism takes the
place of evaluation, however hesitant and embarrassed that evaluation
might be. But some ability to evaluate is necessary. It is a denial of our
responsibility to others to give up on the ability to condemn some
practices and support others.

In so far as post-modernity implies the dulling of the ability to understand and, instead, seems to allow for merely a futile attempt to describe,
so it represents an expression of a confrontation with the sublime. Put
another way, post-modernity can be interpreted in terms of the problem
of the sublime which the modern boundary drawing exercises had
allegedly (and in their own terms not unsuccessfully) solved for the
societal milieu. Of course, the concept of the sublime has a long and
complicated history. The concept has been rarely, if ever, used as a source
of sociological insight. But perhaps it is only through the sublime that it
is possible to even hesitantly come to appreciate what post-modernity
might mean.

Building on Burke, and to a lesser and more critical extent Kant,
Lyotard writes with some clarity: 'Here then is a breakdown of the sublime
sensation: a very big, very powerful object threatens to deprive the soul
of any and all "happenings", stuns it . . . The soul is dumb, immobilized,
as good as dead' (Lyotard 1984: 40). If the post-modern sociality, with its
ceaseless consumption and neo-tribalist plays of surfaces is identified as
a simple fact which can only be registered and described in ethnographies
of the everyday, then it ceases to be intelligible as a process of the
'happening'. It is only that which exists in its dull facticity. There are no
standards by which it is possible to construct the existent as something
which is happening in this way as opposed to that way. It cannot be
explained and assessed in terms of hermeneutic categories and
boundaries. Instead, it is apprehended as too big, as without the bounds
of the understanding. And as such it is spiritually lethal.

The bounded universes called forth by modern sociology might have had disastrous consequences (such as those stressed by Milan Kundera in his story of the European novel). But at least they represented a transcendence of the problem of the sublime. At least they gave a space for freedom and for social and cultural reflection. The modern boundaries provided some way of distancing the societal from the too big and the too powerful world outside of the order of things. The categories of sociology instead rendered the things of the world compatible with the socially and culturally dependent understanding. It might even be said that they made the bounded world beautiful.

It is worth quoting Lyotard again. In the following passage it is also worth substituting the word 'art' with the word 'sociology'. Lyotard is talking about the dangers of the sublime object and he says that: 'Art, by distancing this menace, procures a pleasure of relief, of delight. Thanks to art, the soul is returned to the agitated zone between life and death, and this agitation is its health and its life' (Lyotard 1984: 40). Sociology aspires towards the achievement of much the same end. Of course, one of the instances of this zone of agitation which produces such delight, such relief and yet such panic, is the identified and much expressed conflict between reification and reflexivity. This key myth of modernity is nothing other than an expression of some of the stakes, promises and difficulties of the social and the cultural bounding of the sublime.

The worries and silences which post-modernity intimates are reflections of the confrontation with the sublime. The aporia of post-modernity also intimates nothing other than a possibility of the impossibility of freedom and reflexivity. As Lyotard says, 'the sublime is kindled by the threat that nothing further might happen' (Lyotard 1984: 40). Or, as Lyotard puts it in a comment which can be read as a very precise summary of the reason why the post-modern activities so desperately revolve around ceaseless consumption, and so desperately need to be seen to be doing something: 'Hidden in the cynicism of innovation is surely a despair that nothing further will happen' (Lyotard 1984: 43). And, from the point of view of understanding and interpreting the social, and from the point of view of enhancing the possibilities of freedom in the social world, post-modernity indeed intimates the distinct possibility that nothing else will happen.

But perhaps it is unreasonable to expect anything else to happen. After all, why should anything else happen?

It might be said that, from the post-modern point of view, there is actually nothing left to happen. The last word might indeed have been said. Post-modernity holds out the prospect of the universality of humanity. Of course, the universality is in no small measure a product of the implications of technology and indeed, of the mundane metaphysical wager of immortality. But it remains a universality of a far more likely and practical sort than any of the philosophers were able to imagine in their wildest speculations.

Post-modernity can perhaps be seen as something like the culmination of human history and moreover, as something like the final fulfilment of all of the hopes and ambitions which have been expressed so desperately and so longingly since the birth of philosophy. So long as no attention is paid to the ragged remnants of the pre-historical and the historical who lurk outside the glittering arcades of post-modernity it might seem as if the world has been rendered finally and fully clear. It might well seem as if the mysteries of the world have been solved once and for all. But in any case, what do the dirty and tattered masses mean? From a post-modern point of view, they actually mean nothing because there is nothing for them to mean. All the inhabitants of post-modernity can do now is register their presence. At most they can simply ask the poor what it feels like to be shabby. There is no longer anything that can be done since the presence of the poor no longer implies any social and cultural process of the happening. They are grubby and pathetic and that is all they are.

These are the marks of the sublime post-modernity. It is too big to understand. But perhaps there is no will to understand simply because there is nothing left to understand. There are no more riddles to be solved and no hidden deep truths. After all, for and with post-modernity what you see is what you get. There is nothing more to be said. The dreams of the philosophers might well have been realized. For some people at least there really is no more want, no more need, no more discontent. For some people at least. But that also means that there is no more hope.

To live the post-modern life is to live in the ignorance of the lesson of modernity and specifically the lesson of Franz Kafka that the precondition of hope is the necessary unattainability of that which is hoped for. To live the post-modern life is to live in the truth that the only thing worse than not realizing hopes is actually, to realize them.

Bibliography

Adorno, Theodor W. (1973) *Negative Dialectics*, trans. E.B. Ashton, London: Routledge & Kegan Paul.

—— (1989) 'Perennial Fashion – Jazz', trans. S. and S. Weber, in S.E. Bonner and D.M. Kellner (eds), *Critical Theory and Society. A Reader*, New York: Routledge.

Adorno, Theodor W. and Horkheimer, Max (1972) *Dialectic of Enlightenment*, trans. J. Cumming, New York: Herder and Herder.

Baudrillard, Jean (1983) *In the Shadow of the Silent Majorities*, trans. P. Foss, P. Patton and J. Johnston, New York: Semiotext(e).

Bauman, Zygmunt (1987) *Legislators and Interpreters. On Modernity, Post-modernity and Intellectuals*, Oxford: Polity.

—— (1991) *Modernity and Ambivalence*, Cambridge: Polity.

Beck, Ulrich (1992) 'From Industrial Society to the Risk Society: Questions of Survival, Social Structure and Ecological Enlightenment' *Theory, Culture and Society*, 9(1): 97–123.

Benjamin, Walter (1983) *Charles Baudelaire. A Lyric Poet in the Era of High Capitalism*, trans. H. Zohn, London: Verso.

Berman, Marshall (1983) *All That is Solid Melts into Air. The Experience of Modernity*, London: Verso.

Borges, Jorge Luis (1970) *Labyrinths. Selected Stories and Other Writings*, trans. D.A. Yates and J.E. Irby, Harmondsworth: Penguin.

Chase, Malcolm and Shaw, Christopher (1989) 'The Dimensions of Nostalgia' in C. Shaw and M. Chase (eds), *The Imagined Past. History and Nostalgia*, Manchester: Manchester University Press.

Chaucer, Geoffrey (1951) *The Canterbury Tales*, trans. N. Coghill, Harmondsworth: Penguin

Clark, T.J. (1985) *The Painting of Modern Life. Paris in the Art of Manet and His Followers*, London: Thames & Hudson.

Deleuze, Gilles and Guattari, Felix (1986) *Nomadology: The War Machine*, trans. B. Massumi, New York: Semiotext(e).

Douglas, Mary (1975) *Implicit Meanings. Essays in Anthropology*, London: Routledge & Kegan Paul.

Durkheim, Emile (1952) *Suicide. A Study in Sociology*, trans. J.A. Spaulding and G. Simpson, London: Routledge & Kegan Paul.

—— (1984) *The Division of Labour in Society*, trans. W.D. Halls, Basingstoke: Macmillan.

Eliot, T.S. (1982) *Little Gidding* in P. Porter (ed.), *The Faber Book of Modern Verse*, 4th Edition, London: Faber & Faber.

Engels, Frederick (1942) 'Speech at the Graveside of Karl Marx' in *Karl Marx. Selected Works in Two Volumes*, vol. 1, London: Lawrence & Wishart.

Freud, Sigmund (1961) *Civilization and its Discontents*, New York: W.W. Norton.

Giddens, Anthony (1971) *Capitalism and Modern Social Theory. An Analysis of the Writings of Marx, Durkheim, and Max Weber*, Cambridge: Cambridge University Press.

—— (1990) *The Consequences of Modernity*, Stanford: Stanford University Press.

Goethe, Johann Wolfgang (1949) *Faust. Part One*, trans. P. Wayne, Harmondsworth: Penguin.

Goffman, Erving (1968) *Stigma. Notes on the Management of Spoiled Identity*, Harmondsworth: Penguin.

Gorz, André (1982) *Farewell to the Working Class. An Essay on Post-Industrial Socialism*, trans. M. Sonenscher, London: Pluto.

Gouldner, Alvin W. (1975) 'Prologue to a Theory of Revolutionary Intellectuals' *Telos*, no. 26: 3–36.

—— (1985) *Against Fragmentation. The Origins of Marxism and the Sociology of Intellectuals*, New York: Oxford University Press.

Heidegger, Martin (1978) *Basic Writings*, ed. D. Farrell Krell, London: Routledge & Kegan Paul.

Heller, Agnes (1990) *Can Modernity Survive?* Cambridge: Polity.

Heller, Agnes and Fehér, Ferenc (1988) *The Postmodern Political Condition*, Cambridge: Polity.

Husserl, Edmund (1970) *The Crisis of European Sciences and Transcendental Phenomenology. An Introduction to Phenomenological Philosophy*, trans. D. Carr, Evanston: Northwestern University Press.

Huysmans, Joris-Karl (1952) *Downstream*, trans. R. Baldick, London: The Fortune Press.

—— (1959) *Against Nature*, Harmondsworth: Penguin.

Jonas, Hans (1984) *The Imperative of Responsibility. In Search of an Ethics for the Technological Age*, trans. H. Jonas and D. Herr, Chicago: University of Chicago Press.

Kafka, Franz (1979) *Description of a Struggle and Other Stories*, Harmondsworth: Penguin.

Kant, Immanuel (1963) 'The End of All Things' in *On History*, ed. L.W. Beck, Indianapolis: Bobbs-Merrill.

—— (1970) *Kant's Political Writings*, ed. H. Reiss, Cambridge: Cambridge University Press.

Kundera, Milan (1988) *The Art of the Novel*, trans. L. Asher, London: Faber & Faber.

Levinas, Emmanuel (1988) *The Provocation of Levinas. Rethinking the Other*, ed. R. Bernasconi and D. Wood, London: Routledge.

Lukács, Georg (1991) 'Georg Simmel' *Theory, Culture and Society*, 8(3): 145–50.

Lukes, Steven (1981) 'Fact and theory in the social sciences' in D. Potter (ed.) *Society and the Social Sciences*, London: Open University Press.

Lyotard, Jean François (1984) 'The Sublime and the Avant-Garde' *Art Forum*, April: 36–43.
—— (1989) 'Complexity and the Sublime' in L. Appignanesi (ed.) *Postmodernism. ICA Documents*, London: Free Association Books.
MacIntyre, Alasdair (1985) *After Virtue. A Study in Moral Theory*, Second Edition, London: Duckworth.
Maffesoli, Michel (1988) 'Jeux De Masques: Postmodern Tribalism' *Design Issues*, vol. IV (1–2): 141–51.
—— (1989) (ed.) 'The Sociology of Everyday Life' *Current Sociology*, 37(1).
Marlowe, Christopher (1976) 'Doctor Faustus' in Christopher Marlowe. *Complete Plays and Poems*, ed. E.D. Pendry and J.C. Maxwell, London: Dent.
Marx, Karl (1938) *Capital. A Critical Analysis of Capitalist Production*, vol. 1, London: George Allen & Unwin.
—— (1942) 'Critique of the Gotha Programme' in *Karl Marx. Selected Works in Two Volumes*, vol. 2, London: Lawrence & Wishart.
—— (1973) 'Speech at the Anniversary of the People's Paper' in *Karl Marx, Surveys from Exile. Political Writings Volume 2*, ed. D. Fernbach, Harmondsworth: Penguin.
—— (1973a) 'The British Rule in India' in *Karl Marx. Surveys from Exile. Political Writings Volume 2*, ed. D. Fernbach, Harmondsworth: Penguin.
—— (1977) *Economic and Philosophic Manuscripts of 1844*, Moscow: Progress Publishers.
Marx, Karl and Engels, Frederick (1967) *The Communist Manifesto*, Harmondsworth: Penguin.
—— (1970) *The German Ideology*, ed. C.J. Arthur, London: Lawrence & Wishart.
Mendus, Susan (1989) *Toleration and the Limits of Liberalism*, Basingstoke: Macmillan.
Musil, Robert (1953) *The Man Without Qualities. Volume I*, trans. E. Wilkins and E. Kaiser, London: Secker and Warburg.
Nicholson, Linda J. (ed.) (1990) *Feminism/Postmodernism*, New York: Routledge.
Redner, Harry (1982) *In the Beginning was the Deed. Reflections on the Passage of Faust*, Berkeley: University of California Press.
Rorty, Richard (1989) *Contingency, Irony, and Solidarity*, Cambridge: Cambridge University Press.
Saint-Simon, Henri (1976) *The Political Thought of Saint-Simon*, ed. G. Ionescu, London: Oxford University Press.
Sartre, Jean-Paul (1965) *Nausea*, trans. R. Baldick, Harmondsworth: Penguin.
Schivelbusch, Wolfgang (1980) *The Railway Journey. Trains and Travel in the 19th Century*, trans. A. Hollo, Oxford: Basil Blackwell.
—— (1988) *Disenchanted Night. The Industrialisation of Light in the Nineteenth Century*, trans. A. Davies, Oxford: Berg.
Simmel, Georg (1950) *The Sociology of Georg Simmel*, trans. and ed. K.H. Wolff, New York: The Free Press.
—— (1971) *On Individuality and Social Forms. Selected Writings*, ed. D.N. Levine, Chicago: University of Chicago Press.
—— (1990) *The Philosophy of Money*, trans. T. Bottomore and D. Frisby, Second Edition, London: Routledge.

Skvorecky, Josef (1985) *The Engineer of Human Souls*, trans. P. Wilson, London: Chatto and Windus.

Sontag, Susan (1991) *Illness as Metaphor, and AIDS and its Metaphors*, Harmondsworth: Penguin.

Tester, Keith (1992) *The Two Sovereigns. Social Contradictions of European Modernity*, London: Routledge.

—— (1992a) *Civil Society*, London: Routledge.

Tönnies, Ferdinand (1955) *Community and Association (Gemeinschaft und Gesellschaft)*, trans. C.P. Loomis, London: Routledge & Kegan Paul.

Ure, Andrew (1968) 'Dr Ure on the Philosophy of Manufactures, 1835' in M. Walker (ed.) *Metternich's Europe*, London: Macmillan.

Weber, Max (1930) *The Protestant Ethic and the Spirit of Capitalism*, trans. T. Parsons, London: George Allen & Unwin.

—— (1948) *From Max Weber. Essays in Sociology*, ed. H.H. Gerth and C. Wright Mills, London: Routledge & Kegan Paul.

Williams, Raymond (1973) *The Country and the City*, London: Chatto & Windus.

Williams, Rosalind (1990) *Notes on the Underground. An Essay on Technology, Society, and the Imagination*, Cambridge, Massachusetts: The MIT Press.

Yeats, W.B. (1982) *The Second Coming* in P. Porter (ed.) *The Faber Book of Modern Verse*, fourth Edition, London: Faber & Faber.

Name index

Adorno, T. 17, 76, 94, 98, 122

Baudelaire, C. 132
Baudrillard, J. 35, 51–2, 101
Balzac, H. 16
Bauman, Z. 59, 73, 154
Beck, U. 114–15
Berman, M. 56, 60, 62
Borges, J-L. 124–5, 127–8, 129
Burke, E. 158

Cervantes, M. 15–16, 17, 22
Chaucer, G. 79, 80
Comte, A. 106

Deleuze, G. 75
Diderot, D. 16
Douglas, M. 3–4
Duchamp, M. 32
Durkheim, E. 19, 71–3, 74–5, 76

Elias, N. 78
Eliot, T.S. 10, 121
Engels, F. 24, 25, 40, 41, 45–6, 48–9,
  108–9, 143

Fehér, F. 28, 33, 134–5, 136–7,
  138–40, 143, 149
Flaubert, G. 16
Foucault, M. 48, 140
Freud, S. 20, 31

Giddens, A. 85
Goethe, J.W. 56, 57–60, 66–7

Goffman, E. 144–5
Gorz, A. 35, 49–51
Gouldner, A. 2, 25–6, 35
Gramsci, A. 27
Guattari, F. 75

Heidegger, M. 1, 40, 90–100, 105, 113
Heller, A. 21–2, 28, 33, 134–5,
  136–7, 138–40, 143, 149
Horkheimer, M. 17, 98
Husserl, E. 14–15, 16, 17, 19, 20, 37
Huysmans, J-K. 72, 73, 131–4,
  135–6, 137, 138, 139

Jonas, H. 116–20, 123, 148

Kafka, F. 1, 16, 40, 81–2, 87, 92,
  125, 137, 160
Kant, I. 23–4, 25, 26, 46–7, 54, 58, 59,
  62, 63, 74, 124, 140, 155, 157, 158
Kuhn, T. 26
Kundera, M. 1, 15–17, 20, 22, 24, 37,
  40, 57, 159

Levinas, E. 148
Lukács, G. 13, 17
Lukes, S. 155
Lyotard, J-F. 46, 47, 155–6, 158–9

MacIntyre, A. 129
Maffesoli, M. 76–8, 105, 137–40,
  141, 142
Marlowe, C. 56–7
Marx, K. 13, 14, 17, 24, 25, 34–46,

Subject index